EMPOWERED
BY GOD

EMPOWERED
BY GOD

NANCY MILSK
with Bill Bray

W *Whitaker House*

Unless otherwise noted, Scripture quotations marked (NKJV) are from the *New King James Version*, © 1979, 1980, 1982, 1984 by Thomas Nelson, Inc. Used by permission.

Scripture quotations marked (KJV) are taken from the *King James Version* of the Bible.

Scripture quotations marked (TLB) are from *The Living Bible*, © 1971 by Tyndale House Publishers, Wheaton, Illinois. Used by permission.

EMPOWERED BY GOD

Nancy Milsk
Trumpet Ministries
P.O. Box 2290
Southfield, MI 48037

ISBN: 0-88368-338-5
Printed in the United States of America
Copyright© 1994 by Nancy Milsk and W.T. Bray

Whitaker House
580 Pittsburgh Street
Springdale, PA 15144

Contents

Dedication

This book is dedicated to my husband Charles, who has patiently encouraged me as I found myself becoming a spiritual midwife to the emerging church of the 21st century. Without his quiet support and understanding during these first 25 years of unbelievable outreach, I would never have been able to obey the voice of God and take my place in any kind of Christian ministry.

Foreword

How delightful it is for me to introduce Nancy Milsk's powerful story. First, because I know how hard it is for **anyone** to be called into a special ministry like Nancy's—and all the more so when you're a woman!

I'll never forget my first frustrating attempts to knock on these kinds of closed doors in Taiwan as a young evangelist.

Today, millions of people in Taiwan watch our weekly *Praise the Lord* program. God has allowed my name to become a household word. But it hasn't always been so.

In 1971, when the Lord first called me to start a ministry there, I began by calling on leading clergymen and asking if anyone would like to have me talk in his church.

"Don't you know," they asked sarcastically, "that in China we don't have women evangelists?" "To whom do you belong?" they demanded. "With what ministry are you affiliated—Billy Graham, or Oral Roberts, or what?"

"I belong to Jesus," I told them. "I'm here because He has sent me!"

Sadly for some, both then and now, Jesus just isn't enough. And, of course, this is essentially the same answer that Nancy has given her interrogators over the last twenty years.

For true overcomers like Nancy, there is only one thing to do. You just keep on knocking, and eventually God does open those doors so long closed by the traditions of men. He has opened them for me again and again in Taiwan, on mainland China, and in the USA. And He keeps opening them for Nancy Milsk as well!

Nancy has ministered with us and members of our Nora Lam Team in China and the former Soviet Union, and in many corners of the USA! The Lord has shown me that she is truly a woman of many sorrows, a person who has faced many trials and emerged an overcomer.

This is a great book that every Christian—man or woman, boy or girl—needs to read. **It is for anyone who has ever stood at a door and knocked!**

It's for you, dear believer, if you're crying out today for God to move in your life and situation. If you're waiting for Him to answer the cries of your heart, then crack open this book.

In these pages, you'll see how the Lord has both personal deliverance and revival for you. He'll not only bless you, but use you to bless others. God will do it again. What He's done for so many others, He'll do for you!

God wants you to be an overcomer, and this book will help you find the way to that victory. I believe that Nancy's story will be an encouragement to you as it has been to many others.

Nora Lam
Nora Lam Ministries
San Jose, California

Introduction

How does a suburban housewife from Detroit end up with the courage to go around strategizing with generals, advising presidents, and blessing bishops?

From where does she draw the supernatural audacity to usher in the Holy Spirit of God boldly—not just at church meetings but in hotel lobbies and the halls of government?

It was 2:00 AM when a troubled team member knocked on our hotel room door in Kiev. Deryl asked if I would go check on her roommate. This was on our first mission to the Ukraine with Nancy Milsk—before Communism fell in Russia and the Ukraine was still part of the USSR.

I can still remember her very concerned and worried expression as I peeked out through the tiny crack in our door. It seems her roommate, Nancy Cobb, had gone to learn intercession with Nancy Milsk and Jacque Heasley.

Strange things were going on—and the missing roommate had been absent for hours. The worry and fear in Deryl's voice was real enough to make me think that maybe something was actually physically wrong.

So pulling on my clothes, I told my wife I'd be right back and walked back down the hall with Deryl, still in my bare feet. She pointed me toward Nancy's room and ducked back into her own. As I came closer, I began to understand why there was such panic in her voice.

God at Work in Willing Hearts

From behind the door, I heard groans and shrieks that sounded like the emergency room of an Army field hospital. I timidly knocked on the door, more than a little afraid of what I might find. Perhaps one of the women had gotten food poisoning and needed a doctor.

The door swung open. Nancy and her two breathless companions—embarrassed to be seen in curlers without their makeup—stood there with radiant faces. They glowed through a shiny film of sweat, proof positive of how very hard they were working at prayer. Whatever was going on, the presence of God was very obvious from the ecstasy in their eyes. I knew there was nothing wrong. But I also sensed that something was going on in the spiritual world which I didn't understand.

Nancy wordlessly tugged me into the room, pushed me into a chair, and resumed groaning in fervent, noisy prayer. It was the first time I had ever witnessed such physical, birthing intercession. Jacque Heasley fell on her knees and curled into a fetal position on the floor, grabbing her stomach with a series of cries and gasps that sounded like she was actually in a maternity ward!

In a split-second, the Holy Spirit revealed to me what was going on, and I began to draw back in fear and wonder. These women were travailing in prayer, literally delivering spiritual babies! By prayer, they were casting down communist idols and liberating the Ukraine from Soviet domination.

Prevailing, Travailing Prayer

The room seemed so feminine. I felt I had intruded into a distinctly woman's experience in intercession and prophecy—which of course is not true. However, few men seem to have the patience to wait for this kind of prayer or even know that such intensity in prayer is available to them.

After all, having never personally experienced physically giving birth, men are at a disadvantage when it comes to learning how to give birth in the Spirit. I felt almost sexually embarrassed to be there, yet curious. And frankly, I was a little afraid that if I remained in the room my turn to travail might be next!

My fears were well justified. The Bible says that there are indeed times of trial when men do travail. *"So why do I see every man with his hands on his loins, like a woman in labor, and all faces turned pale?"* (Jeremiah 30:6). I was soon to learn that in the spiritual realm, God breaks yokes and bursts bonds as men join women in prevailing prayer, sharing the pangs of spiritual birth.

God Answers Obedient Prayer

Only a year later, I returned to Kiev on another mission and saw the result of their travail. I was astonished to find revival spreading throughout the Ukraine. Even in the smallest villages, churches and home groups were reforming after decades without a public witness.

The dread KGB headquarters was being used for church services. Sunday school was being held in rooms where believers had once been tortured for Christ. The huge Communist Party Headquarters was boarded up and guarded by Ukrainian troops!

"October Revolution Square" in downtown Kiev had been renamed "Independence Square." I arrived in time to see vandals pulling down idols of Lenin and Marx—images that had enslaved the Ukraine for over 70 years.

What they didn't know, of course, was that a group of women had already pulled down those idols in the spirit. A year before, I had watched and listened as Nancy prophesied against the spiritual powers that held Kiev captive. She had loosed the city for God first in the spiritual realm!

Who Will Join God's Army?

What would happen if more believers learned to practice the secrets of this kind of prayer and prophecy? Where are those willing to go into the Holy of Holies and come out with God's plan for healing cities, families and nations?

Global Mapping in Colorado has pinpointed 6,600 people groups or "nations" which still must receive a gospel witness before Christ can return for His bride. Who will pray and speak the will of God into existence for these people?

But the need for such a fresh move of God is not limited to the mission fields. Too often Christian leaders and parents seem powerless to respond to the tidal wave of secular materialism and compromise sweeping our land today.

Our families, government, mass media and schools are in unprecedented crisis. Church services have all too often degenerated into mere ritual at the very moment we need to see God intervene the most.

When Prayer Alone Is Not Enough

Usually it isn't enough to simply pray. Action is needed. God must move. Prophetic, listening prayer births new vision and faith for divine intervention. As the prophetic word goes out, the move of God begins.

Nancy Milsk has learned the secret of taking her place in this kind of creative intercession. It belongs to the body of Christ today as it has in past ages. End-time prophets are needed now to bring in a fresh move of God.

Maybe you are one of them. In the pages that follow, you can find out. With that prayer in our hearts, we present Nancy's own story. Except for an occasional name change to preserve someone's privacy, everything in this book actually happened. We hope the retelling will help you discover your part in God's end-times move.

Bill Bray
Co-author

Part One:

"In Jerusalem"

But you shall receive power when the Holy Spirit has
come upon you; and you shall be witnesses to Me
in Jerusalem, *and in all Judea and Samaria,*
and to the end of the earth.
—Acts 1:8

In the late 1960s and into the turbulent 1970s, millions of housewives and mothers across North America began to search for God in a new way. This spiritually hungry army began discovering each other and networked into small groups to reach out to their local communities, their "Jerusalems." They used their only discretionary hours from 9:00 AM to 3:00 PM to pray, study, worship and explore the power of God.

Students of revival now look back and realize that this phenomenal awakening grew into one of the greatest moves of God in the 20th century. It crossed cultural, denominational, gender, and racial barriers to circle the globe. Millions found Christ.

Secular media labeled it many ways. They called it the "born-again movement," the "Jesus people," the "evangelical age," or the "charismatic renewal."

In this move of God, Nancy not only found Christ as her living Lord, but learned to birth it into her world. It was the start of a lifelong ministry behind the scenes of God's global stage.

Chapter 1

Billy Graham Is Coming to Town!

*Now faith is the substance of things hoped for, the
evidence of things not seen...by faith we understand that
the worlds were framed by the word of God.*
—Hebrews 11:1,3

From my seat in Deck 3, Row 27, Billy Graham could
barely be seen far below. He looked like a child's toy
soldier. God was answering prayer right before my eyes,
but it still seemed strangely unreal.

Something was wrong in my heart. Was this all
there was to the great event? I had worked so hard for
tonight and waited for years. My thoughts were mixed
with the salty taste of bitter, uncontrollable tears.

My husband Charles couldn't understand why I
wasn't celebrating. Neither could I, really. I came to
watch a great harvest of souls turning to God—and glory
a little in my success! Instead, I sat weeping among the
crowd. My stomach was wrenched by cramping, dull
pains—the kind between labor-room contractions.

I felt guilt at this inability to turn off the tears and
pain. The Lord had answered five years of unwavering

faith. Travailing prayer brought miracle after miracle. The cynics were wrong. Billy Graham was here at last!

Why wasn't I basking in a "told-you-so" victory? Why couldn't I just praise the Lord and shake these feelings of incompleteness and disappointment? Why was I experiencing these emotions of rejection and self-pity? They were so strong and unexpected.

God Visits Motown!

Traffic outside the immense stadium was jammed with cars and buses backed up for miles. The brand new Pontiac Silverdome boasted of having 23,000 parking spaces. Every one seemed full that cold October night!

It was the largest crowd I'd ever seen anywhere for anything. This epiphany was the greatest evangelistic event in Detroit history. About 80,000 came nightly to hear Graham preach the hope of salvation to a city of despair. Detroit was then the racially troubled murder capital of the world.

The giant stadium was packed with people of every race, religion and culture. Hundreds of nationalities sat peacefully together to hear Christ's promise of an even greater peace—peace with God.

For once, the throbbing energy of Motown had ground to halt. The crowd hushed. It was so silent, as if even the big auto-assembly lines were stopping for the Lord. Hundreds of chartered buses from the inner city and the suburbs filled the lots nightly.

The View from Stadium Heaven

Though we finally found one of the few seats left, in the highest tier, I didn't dare remove my sunglasses. I needed them to hide bloodshot eyes and runny mascara. The tears came even more uncontrollably.

I pouted and offered my sacrifice of praise, alternately awed and embittered by the crowd around me. I tried hard to lighten up, to joke with Charles about our seats in "stadium heaven." The words turned to cotton in my mouth.

Confused and helpless to provide comfort for my mysterious grief, he in turn tried his best to cheer me up. This wasn't hormones. Taking an aspirin didn't make it go away. It was in my spirit, and I couldn't explain why I was so anguished.

I fled to the bathroom to cry alone some more and fix my makeup. "What's the matter, God?" I cried. "Why am I like this?"

Christ Himself spoke to my spirit, *"Nancy, I'm now allowing you to feel what I feel for the lost souls of Detroit. Won't you tarry with Me one more hour?"*

"Oh, yes, Lord!" I sighed. "But I don't understand what's happening to me. Why do I still have to travail? Isn't it over yet? Haven't I already done my part?"

Christ's Passion in the Silverdome

Christ's words from John 16:21 came to my mind, *"A woman, when she is in labor, has sorrow because her hour has come; but as soon as she has given birth to the child, she no longer remembers the anguish, for joy that a human being has been born into the world."*

Then God spoke, *"This is what the passion of My death and resurrection are all about, Nancy. This is why I answered the prayers of My people and sent Billy Graham to Detroit.*

"You are sharing in the mystery of spiritual birth today. Therefore, you have sorrow. You weep and lament, but the world rejoices. You are sorrowful now, but your sorrow will turn to joy!"

Suddenly the rest of John 16 began to come back to me: the parts about the tribulation we would have in this world, and the tremendous prayer promise that *"whatever you ask the Father in My name He will give you"* (v. 23).

All this made sense if I were called into a ministry that shares vicariously in Christ's suffering, one that feels His unquenchable thirst for the lost souls He died to save. Was God calling me to this? Why hadn't anyone ever told me about this secret ministry?

My work wasn't over yet. It wasn't enough to get the crusade started. Christ wanted me to stay with Him to the end, praying and delivering these souls from death to life, from darkness to light through prayer. The birthing wasn't complete yet. No wonder my tears couldn't stop.

The Dark Side of My Feelings

Part of the mystery was explained, but there was also a less noble side of my emotions. Christ was also dealing with that. Unless I could learn to handle it, I would be useless in my calling.

You see, besides the spiritual birth pangs, I was suffering another of Christ's sorrows—rejection of men. But unlike my Lord, I was having a hard time forgiving. The trouble with this kind of bitterness is that it won't just lie there and rot. It's like a zombie that keeps rising from the grave in a horror movie!

I had to learn to accept rejection as part of my identification with Christ, the *"man of sorrows"* who was betrayed by those he came to save. I couldn't forgive the official "Billy Graham parade" for marching on and leaving me behind.

Every few minutes, flames of rage would rise in my throat, angry fires which I swallowed back down again. I was too ladylike to act out these nasty, fleshly emotions. If I only had the courage, the hurt little girl in me would have stood up and shouted, "Hey, look at me! I'm Nancy Milsk, and I helped start this whole thing. I invited Billy Graham to Detroit! Don't you remember my story in *The Tribune?*"

Even though I knew this horrible wounded pride was childish—and I hated myself for feeling it—I wasn't yet able to release this my pain to the Lord. I nursed memories of the mailings, the visits, the petitions and the hundreds of phone calls which I had personally made. I recounted every dollar we had spent and recalled countless hours of work invested in launching the crusade.

Fondling the Pain

Embracing the hurt, I rehearsed memories of the slights, the sneers and the backbiting of those who had opposed us, some of whom were right now sitting on the platform in their clerical collars! I tried to imagine Christ hating their hypocrisy as I did, but suddenly I felt very alone. The Lord was not there to empathize with my unforgiving judgments.

That little girl in me went on pouting. "Imagine, Billy Graham is finally here because you got the ball rolling, and you're not even invited to meet him! You were the one who kept the drums beating for a Graham crusade when everyone else thought it impossible. Now the crusade is on and you're not even getting an honorable mention."

There was some truth in all my whining. A host of demons were on hand to point this out. I was not just feeling completely and totally forgotten—I really had been dismissed!

God's Reluctant, Invisible Woman

"Nobody appreciates me anymore," I agreed with the devil's hosts. "Here I sit, just another face in the crowd, in the worst seat in the house. No one shook my hand when I came in or even had a kind word of thanks. I was not invited backstage or given a special seat on the platform. It's like I don't even exist!

"Not even an usher recognizes me. To them I'm like everyone else, a nobody! There wasn't a line of type about us in the program." I was fuming inside. I had become the invisible woman in this effort, and I didn't like the anonymity one bit.

Charles tried as best he could to console me, but at that terrible moment I was simply beyond human comfort. Even if my businessman husband had been able to tell me about Jonah sulking outside the walls of Nineveh or Elijah's depression in the cave of Mt. Horeb, I wasn't yet ready to listen to any kind of reason or counsel. Right then, I was sulking—and secretly enjoying every minute of my miserable pity-party.

"For whom the Lord loves He chastens."

Although I was too young in Christ to understand yet, God was lovingly applying my first serious spanking in the Christian ministry. In Hebrews 12:6, Scripture says that we must endure chastening with patience, *"for whom the Lord loves He chastens and scourges every son whom He receives."*

He had received me as His child. Now, He was allowing some emotional pain in order to get through to me. I was learning one of the most important lessons ever about the nature of my calling in Christ. But just then, the logic and benefit of the Lord's discipline was incomprehensible.

Like a child in a tantrum, I just knew one thing: I wasn't getting my way. It wasn't fair, and I didn't like it. Although God in His grace had greatly used me, in many ways I was proving that I was still very much a spiritual infant.

The Work of the Cross in Our Ministries

But thank God the cross of Christ was starting to work in my life and ministry. This was many years before John Dawson wrote his book, *Taking Our Cities for God*, but he has described well what I was going through:

> Self-interest, self-promotion, self-preservation and self-consciousness have to die for us to experience intimate friendship with a holy God and to obtain overcoming authority in destroying the works of Satan.
> (Dawson, 1989, Creation House, p. 213)

That such unrewarded or unrecognized ministry could actually be a calling of God was nowhere in my script! I hadn't yet learned that I was an "anointer" in the body of Christ. Like Samuel, I had to identify and call out others to His service. More often than not, such ministries as mine serve anonymously, behind the scenes.

There are "kings" and "king-makers" in the kingdom of God. The intercessors and prophets are really the king-makers. In American society, pastors and evangelists have become the kings.

The Loneliest Call of All

I didn't know yet that ministries like mine play a supporting rather than starring role in the drama of God's move. It would take some years to learn and re-learn this first basic truth about my ministry, but the lesson began that night in "stadium heaven."

The gifts of intercession and prophecy are "mothering ministries." They are barely visible callings, but they mobilize and give life to all the others! They work best when they are unseen. By their very definition and nature, they are prelude. It is no surprise to find they are so often taken for granted, private, unnoticed, unrewarded, without acclaim or applause.

Intercession is the loneliest call of all. It is the ministry of conception. I know intercessors who simply stand outside abortion clinics—not to protest the murders or block women from entering—but simply to pray silently. Prayer is action.

Prophecy goes further then intercession, but it always begins in prayer. It gives birth to a new move of God. It articulates a judgment of God or clarifies a need. Often, the prophet must also perform this calling unseen, behind closed doors.

One top leader in Africa recently testified, "Nancy, God sent you all the way here just for me." It would not surprise me at all to find out in heaven that he was right.

The image of a street-corner prophet with a sign that reads, "The End Is Near," may be great fun for cartoonists, but it almost never happens in real life. Rarely does prophetic insight come publicly or to the masses. Most often the prophet delivers the pregnant word to one or two key leaders, a committee or a small congregation.

Ministry in the Secret Place

Not only does the spotlight rarely focus on prophets, but they are seldom welcome by those in authority! I have yet to see a king or leader roll out the red carpet when a prophet appears—either in the church or the world. Pulpits and platforms rarely open to prophets—and even less so to women. Those with governing gifts rightfully fear that their agendas may be altered or sins exposed.

Often, the prophet's message is not even understood. It is received with fear, hatred and mistrust. No wonder the *"prophet's reward"* (Matthew 10:41) throughout history has all too often been exile, prison or death.

But I was still learning and could barely understand all this, even when the Lord himself spoke words of comfort and explanation to me later that night.

I thank the Lord for giving me a husband understanding enough to sit back and let the Holy Spirit have His way with me. Charles just sat there while I sniffled through most of the service. Like all the big lessons on our spiritual journeys, this one had to be learned in my own soul. Before the night ended, the Lord turned my agony into ecstasy, and I understood why.

Taking Our City for God

The thrill of conceiving and giving birth to the Billy Graham Crusade began in 1972. The violence of the 1967 Detroit race riots was still very fresh in our minds. Mob rule, drugs and prostitution were replacing the brand names of automobile manufacturers as the "real" trademarks of our city. Metro Detroit was the archetypal rustbelt example of urban corruption and decay, sinking into economic crisis.

Angela Davis, a controversial Afro-American militant, was in town, offering angry, violent solutions to our worsening race relations. Our church was supporting her at the time, although her rhetoric was producing only more hatred and bloodshed.

I met Marilyn Flora at a women's Bible study at Northbrook Presbyterian Church in Birmingham. After the meeting had ended, I sat with Marilyn in her cherry-colored Nova talking about Angela's message and the spiritual sickness that was gripping Detroit. She suddenly turned to me and said, "Nancy, if you're going to do anything for God, you must do it now!"

Marilyn had goals, gave orders, took charge. She was a woman on a mission for God, moving with a sense of destiny. She was just what I needed.

Her words were anointed with prophetic authority. They were like one of those tractor beams on Star Trek, fastening onto me and dragging me forward. I sensed immediately that God was speaking. His call was irresistible. I was a brand-new, baby Christian. Her words of challenge rang in my ears like God's commission to the prophet in Isaiah 6, or the Lord's charge to *"feed my sheep"* in John 21.

God Confirms My Call in Scripture

I underlined both passages in my new *Living Bible*. Her words were drawing me into some kind of ministry which I couldn't define, one that I didn't see modeled in any church, but which I knew was a calling from God.

In fact, almost from the very day of my conversion, I had felt the Lord calling me to some unspoken purpose—His divine purpose for the life of Nancy Milsk. It was as if my surrender to the grace of God was both for salvation and service. The crack of light between them was so narrow that I didn't even see it.

I remember sitting at my typewriter, starting to write my first letters begging Billy Graham to come to Detroit, when the Lord spoke to me clearly from John 21:15-17. He simply said, *"Do you love Me? Then feed My sheep!"*

Silence followed as the room stood still around me in the Holy presence of God. Again, His question to Peter was repeated, *"Do you love Me?"*

"Is it really you, Lord?" I asked in wonder.

His only reply came again, *"Feed My sheep."*

"Feed My sheep," repeated Christ for the third time. It really was the Lord. He had confirmed Marilyn's charge to me, just as He had to Peter.

The Billy Graham Miracle

Those troubled Detroit days demanded a big event—a dramatic pronouncement of the Gospel that would reach all for Christ. As young Christians, a Billy Graham Crusade seemed the obvious and only choice, but we had no idea of how difficult it was to stage such an enormous and expensive event.

If we knew in 1972 what we would know by 1976, we would never have started. We were just two housewives with families to raise, from the wrong side of town, without connections, and from the wrong denomination. We didn't even know that there were spiritual gifts, let alone understand what our gifts were! And if we had, we wouldn't have known how to use them. The charismatic movement was just starting to sweep the country.

Even worse, we didn't know anything about demonic forces or spiritual warfare, about taking cities for God or breaking down spiritual strongholds. We had never heard anything about territorial spirits or seen miracles of God's intervention.

Finally, we were up against a race war. We were white women in a city where the power was shifting into the hands of angry black men who had been oppressed for over a century.

Nothing Is Impossible with God

But none of these things on the long list of impossibilities mattered to us—or to God! We instinctively knew that Detroit needed the good news of His Gospel to free us from hopeless decay. We believed God was calling us to action. In the end, that's all that mattered!

After my conversion, Marilyn and I soon found our simple belief that "Christ was the answer for Detroit" to be a joke at our church. For these church women, collecting canned goods was the definition of acceptable evangelism. This form of witnessing through "presence" and "acts of compassion" was all they knew—and the farthest extent to which they were willing to go. The idea that preaching the Gospel was the engine that drives all social change was greeted with embarrassed chuckles.

But for five years we sounded only one note: "Billy Graham is coming to Detroit!" We worked for it. We spoke for it. We prayed for it daily. It was our watchword, our crazy cause: "Billy Graham is coming to town!"

Chapter 2

Born-again Woman

Do not marvel that I said unto you,
You must be born again.
—John 3:7

I broke out of my religious traditions to become a born-again Christian in February, 1970. It happened at one of the dozens of women's Bible studies that were then in vogue in suburban Detroit. Almost every church had one; they had become like a Junior League for church women.

Some of the groups were little more than bridge clubs, but the angel of the Lord was stirring the waters anyway. There was growing spiritual expectancy in the air. Many were going beyond the tea-party stage to explore the Lordship of Christ in their lives. The groups sprang up all over, organized by hungry women who yearned for a spiritual reality they generally did not find elsewhere. It was a super-charged spiritual environment.

Charles and I had been married in 1957. By 1970 our three children were all school age. He was doing well in my father-in-law's electronics business. I didn't have to go back to work unless I wanted to—and I didn't! The American dream had come true for me. I was just a middle-class girl from South Oakland—not rich, but affluent enough to stay home if I wanted.

I discovered "mother's hours" from 9 to 3 weekdays. It was a *kairos* moment, a "fullness of time." At last I had a quiet space to be able to reflect on life. Without the kids underfoot every moment with their demands and needs, I began thinking about my spiritual longings again, something I hadn't done since my early teens.

These were also the salad days of the women's movement. Many of my friends were using their newly-found liberation to get jobs, but I knew this would not fill the emptiness in my heart.

We were faithful church-goers with the "socially acceptable amount of religion" for our community—but I was no longer satisfied with just playing church.

If Charles and I weren't exactly the pillars of our church, at least we tried to be! I even attempted to teach Sunday school for awhile. This was a real-life example of the blind leading the blind. I soon found I couldn't teach about a lifestyle I didn't have.

Nothing filled that void inside, including my ever-more-frequent shopping trips to the new malls that were popping up everywhere. I loved my jewelry, fine fashions and silks. But even the most beautiful and glamorous fabrics too quickly lost their luster.

Although Charles and I were busy planning our next move up to a "real" dream house, inside I was already tired of keeping up with the Joneses. Somehow, I knew in advance that the things of this world were never going to satisfy my real needs.

Shopping for God

So, without talking about it with the family, I instinctively searched for a Savior. I didn't know why, but my present relationship with God was not working.

Most of all, I wanted Him to be intimate and real in my everyday life. God was watching me from a distance, but He was nowhere near enough for me to touch. So, although I couldn't articulate my needs, I decided to go shopping for God.

There were lots of places to look for Him. The spiritual fluttering in my soul drove me to start secretly visiting daytime Bible studies, sometimes three or four days a week. Each was at a different church or home.

The first was at our home church. It was a Christian social club, intellectual and charitable. Speakers shared about politically correct subjects and social concerns. The first assumption of the group was that we were all okay, loved and accepted by God.

I wanted to talk about God, but somehow it seemed impolite to talk about the Lord or our relationship with Him. Any mention of our sins and the Savior was taboo. We started a discussion group to study the Bible and other books—but nothing that was said or done satisfied my growing spiritual thirst.

That's when I started visiting other groups.

Something Different in the Air

One very cold day in February, I tried the women's luncheon at Highland Park Baptist. There I found Christ as Lord and Savior. After years of church attendance and faithfully practicing Christian religion, I finally met the Founder of the Faith.

Jesus said in John 10 that His sheep hear His voice and follow Him. I guess I was the little lost lamb at that time. I didn't even know that I knew the sound of His voice, but I recognized Him as soon as I heard it!

Walking into Highland Park Baptist, I sensed something different. It wasn't the place or the program, but the people. The women I met were alive, loving and genuinely concerned about me. They had vibrant spiritual lives that showed. I knew they knew Him in a way I didn't. I wanted what they obviously had, a direct connection to God.

My Faith Mentor

I remember wearing my favorite yellow sheath with a pretty matching scarf that day. Elizabeth MacDonald spotted me and strolled across the room in welcome. For some reason, I was not surprised later when she turned out to be the speaker. Her relaxed confidence was impressive.

She carried herself with easy elegance—something which up until then I felt was impossible to find at a Christian women's meeting! Always clothes-conscious, I knew from the way she dressed that she had money. That made her religious faith all the more interesting to me! It came as no surprise later to find out that she was the wife of Ford's Vice President for new product development.

But more than anything else, Elizabeth captured my attention through her boldness for God. She spoke of the Lord as if He lived just next door, as if she talked with Him everyday when she went out to get the morning paper! She was very verbal about her faith and sure of her relationship with God.

God Rings My Bell

Inside, a little bell began ringing. She had it! I knew she had it—peace with God! My heart cried out to share the same certainty. Would it ever be possible for me to know God like that? I was curious as to how she had developed such trust in Him. Was it really possible to know God that intimately? Was this some kind of act she was putting on, or was her spiritual life for real?

As we sat eating seashell macaroni and tuna fish salad with plastic spoons from paper plates, I was fascinated by the way she described the Lord. Her intimacy with Him was so different from my head knowledge of God. I had memorized the Apostles' Creed and repeated it all the time. That was my kind of faith. I thought I believed in Christ, but when I listened to Elizabeth I began to have increasing doubts. Somehow, my intellectual assent to a creed on Sunday and her trust in Christ were not the same.

When Elizabeth was introduced as the speaker, she left her mink stole on the seat next to me and strolled confidently forward. I sensed this grace was no act of pretense. I was seeing her exactly as she was.

As she witnessed, I realized I was hearing the unvarnished story of her personal journey without any apology. It spoke straight from her heart to mine.

Women like Marabel Morgan, who later wrote *The Total Woman*, were just starting to make the speaking circuit in those days. The subject of submission was a hot topic. Soon Elizabeth had us all in hilarious laughter as she recalled her attempts to be submissive to her husband—no easy task for such a strong-willed woman. Nobody ever accused Elizabeth of being a wimpy doormat! Once, after her conversion, in a dramatic gesture of self-righteous witnessing, she poured her husband's prized collection of aged Scotch whiskey down the toilet!

As she related her struggle to witness and live for Christ in the elite corporate world at Ford Motors, we were easily able to find parallels in our own worlds. I sensed that others in the room were experiencing the same response. We were all somewhere on a journey to find God. We were trying to define Christian relationships in the midst of the materialism and militant feminism that were sweeping the country.

Back then, we were all still feeling pretty good about ourselves. No one had even heard of AIDS yet, and the sexual revolution was going full blast. Women's magazines all held out hope for a future without glass ceilings —one where we all realized our full potential, having our cake and eating it, too.

The hedonism of the sixties had not completely turned into the greedy materialism of the eighties yet. The Vietnam War was spending itself, and the Playboy generation was still healthy, wealthy and wise. But something was desperately wrong just below the surface of our lives. Though it wasn't chic to admit it openly, we were all on a search for spiritual answers.

Elizabeth seemed to have found those answers to my unformed spiritual questions. She was boldly incorporating Christ into career, marriage, home and family— successfully achieving the same goals I wanted in my life.

A Long-forgotten Voice

I was on my feet in a heartbeat when she closed her talk by asking us all to stand and pray if we wanted to be born again. I didn't really understand what being born again meant. Until then, I had only heard the term used in ridicule. But now I was standing with several other housewives, asking to have a personal rebirth in Christ.

"Do I really need to do this, Lord?" I prayed.

"Yes," said a voice I hadn't heard for years, *"Go for it!"* It was the Lord. I was hearing Him speak to me for the first time in my adult life. It was as if my spirit were being awakened from a long sleep. I recognized that I

hadn't talked with this voice since I was a schoolgirl —maybe even since childhood.

"Go for it," said the voice of God again.

How could I have forgotten the sound of that voice in my heart? When did I stop listening to God? I couldn't remember the moment, but I realized that no one can hear it who is not willing to become a child again.

And so "go for it" I did. I came back to Wednesday luncheon every week. Each time, they invited people to accept Christ. And each and every time I stood up and prayed that same prayer! I invited Christ into my life over and over again those first weeks.

"Lord Jesus," I repeated with all the sincerity I could muster, "I believe You died for me. I confess I am a sinner. Come into my heart and be my Lord. Amen."

I really got it down! I didn't understand the finality of my decision until some sensitive, mature women in the fellowship took me under their spiritual wings and began to disciple me. I especially remember Ruth Duff and Nellie Pickard. They loved the Word of God and introduced me to the Bible as a map for my spiritual life.

God's Love Letter to Me

After the weekly luncheon, I started going home with these older women where they patiently answered questions about God. About that time, somebody gave me a copy of *The Living Bible*, a paraphrased edition of the Scriptures by Ken Taylor. It helped me get beyond the archaic translation of my *King James Version*. I started to understand the Bible for the first time.

Somebody wisely advised me to start my Scripture study by reading the Gospel of John five times. It was the best counsel anyone could have given me. Reading

John over and over, my relationship with Christ as the Son of God and Savior was finally established.

The Bible, which had been so dead to me before, suddenly burned like fire! It was His love letter to me. I read it as eagerly as any schoolgirl with her first crush. Each word of the Bible seemed to come alive and speak. How could I have missed all this truth before?

I continued to attend the women's group at my church. That was still my home base. I gradually became confident about sharing my new discovery of faith with anybody there who would listen.

Surprising Challenges

Not everyone liked it. I was stunned to find most of the women at our home church were embarrassed by my new zeal and felt I needed a quick prescription of Valium! For the first time in my life, I was sure of my salvation and my growing relationship with Christ. But instead of rejoicing with me, I was hurt that my so-called Christian friends did everything they could to challenge my newfound joy.

"What about the Hindus and the Muslims?" they argued at my Tuesday group. "Aren't they sincere in their faith, too? How can you be so sure that you're so okay with God? What about them? They have many wonderful truths in their religions!"

It was a strange line of questioning I hadn't expected from Christians. I knew that God loved people of all religions and that Christ died for everyone and wanted all to be saved, but I didn't have an answer for them. The next day, I found myself rushing to Ruth and Nellie at Highland Park with this question, the first of many that would follow.

"Salvation is not about sincerity or religion," they answered. They turned to John 14:6 and read, *"Jesus said to him, 'I am the way, the truth and the life. No man comes to the Father but by me.'"*

"No matter how faithful we are to our religion, only Christ can take away our sin and reconcile us with God. That's why Christ instructed that we witness to all the world with the Gospel, delivering the salvation message of God's love to everyone."

I was satisfied. With John 14:6 underlined in my Bible, I went back to my Tuesday fellowship. But I barely had shared the answer to their question when I found myself challenged from another angle.

"Well," sneered one self-righteous sister, "it's not as easy as you think. You just don't believe and get saved! The Bible says, *'Faith without works is dead'* (James 2:20). Belief alone isn't enough—you have to have good works, too."

Cornered again, I rushed back to Ruth and Nellie. We studied the book of Galatians where Paul deals in depth with the relationship of faith and works. I learned that good works and holiness come naturally in a growing Christian life. They are legitimate evidences of faith, a result of the Holy Spirit working within us. But that doesn't mean we are saved by our works, *"for by grace you have been saved through faith, and that not of yourselves: it is the gift of God, not of works, lest anyone should boast"* (Ephesians 2:8-9).

"All have sinned and come short of the glory of God" (Romans 3:23). No amount of good works can eliminate our sin. Even the best Christian is a sinner who needs daily forgiveness. In this case, the bumper sticker is right: "Christians aren't perfect, they're just forgiven."

I came back and read Ephesians 2:8-9 to the Tuesday group. No matter how many times I would explain this concept, or come back with testimonies of how my neighbors were now discovering the power of faith, I found that most of the women in my Tuesday group were unable to grasp this idea.

Free grace and faith were a stumbling block to their religion of good works. Because of this, their walks with God were stunted and deformed. Their spiritual powers were limited to only what they could handle in the strength of the flesh.

God's power is unlocked only by faith. So for these religious women of unbelief, God was confined to the limits imposed by their human abilities, intellects, love and resources. When the fiery darts of the enemy were thrown at most of their lives, their human shields failed.

But this wasn't true for all of them. Marilyn Flora was one who had heard the call of faith. Everywhere—in the most fashionable downtown church or in the worst prison—God has a remnant. Marilyn and I soon discovered each other as spiritual sisters. We began knocking on heaven's doors, asking God for more of everything He had for us.

My First Moses

Marilyn Flora was my first spiritual Moses. I became her Aaron as we studied together and eventually took on Detroit as our mission field. Marilyn gave drive and leadership, while I was able to articulate and write out her vision. Together with an intercessory prayer warrior, Ann Avesian, we made up the trio of ladies that began to believe God for a Billy Graham Crusade to be held in greater Detroit.

No social climber, Marilyn was content to live with her husband and one child in a two-bedroom Ferndale house, just inside Detroit. At least ten years my senior, she was on a mission for God 24 hours a day. There was an urgency to all she did. Dressed in an unfashionable fake leopard-skin coat and plastic "go-go boots" left over from the '60s, she was aflame and militant for the Lord.

Marilyn was another Bible-study gypsy, traveling from group to group in order to get fed. She couldn't get enough. In fact, while we were driving from one Bible study to another, she issued the Billy Graham challenge to me. It became a four-year battle cry in our efforts to bring the crusade to Detroit.

She was to repeat it again and again in the months that followed. "Now look, you guys, if you want to do something for God, now is the time to do it!" (None of us knew of course, how especially prophetic this statement was for Marilyn. She went to be with the Lord soon after the Billy Graham Crusade—a victim of ovarian cancer.)

This was the first time I ever met someone so consumed with love. It was not hard to imagine her standing atop the Renaissance Tower in downtown Detroit, weeping for our city as Jesus wept for Jerusalem. She loved the people of the city and felt a heavy burden for all who suffered there—Anglos, Africans, Hispanics and the scores of ethnic groups that make up our diverse population.

Enlisting "Star Power" for God

She was also practical enough to knew we needed a bigger-than-life celebrity spokesperson to attract the attention of Detroit. We needed a religious superstar. "Billy Graham is like a movie star, an attraction," she proclaimed one day. "He's the only man in America who can get us together and make all Detroit listen—the suburbs as well as the inner city."

Her logic made sense to me. Without questioning, I followed her example and began praying, writing letters and talking to anyone who would listen about the need to have a Billy Graham Crusade in Detroit. I sent out so many mailings that we burned out my father-in-law's copying machine! Once, we mailed 1,600 hand-addressed postcards to every pastor in the Detroit Council of Churches Directory.

Not knowing anything about church politics and denominations, we jumped in our cars and just started "cold calling" without any introductions. My husband is a salesman, so I just went out like he would. Naively, we knocked on every ecclesiastical door we discovered, from "flaming liberals" to "fighting fundies." We visited the mansions of High Church bishops in the day and store-front missions at night. Not having any idea of who would help and who wouldn't, we treated charismatic Catholic convents and Plymouth Brethren Bible chapels with equal seriousness.

I can't remember that we ever stopped to think how it would be possible for us to fund, organize or staff a multi-million dollar Billy Graham Crusade. We only knew somehow Christ was directing us, and we had to obey in faith.

Marilyn and I worked together like Mary and Elizabeth in Luke 1:41. Elizabeth said her baby leaped within her womb, already recognizing that Mary was carrying Emmanuel. That's how it was with both of us. We didn't really know what was happening, but we both knew that we had divine life within us and somehow that life was mysteriously connected.

It was good for me to start out my Christian service in this way. My first experience in ministry was a perfect example of blind faith and obedience converging. When God is truly in control it's like that—wonderfully scary.

You don't really know what's coming next. You simply have to trust the Lord one day at a time for each step.

Knowing what I know today, I probably would never have joined Marilyn in this wild venture for Christ. But then, we wouldn't have been able to bring Billy Graham to Detroit. Only a fool for Christ would have tried what we did. However, that's the way spiritual breakthroughs and revivals almost always come.

Getting Clout for God

"Who are you, lady?" challenged the Bishop as I urged him to invite Graham.

Another skeptical super-pastor gave us the break-through advice that actually did get the crusade in motion. "Listen," he said irritably, "you need some real clout before I can bring this to our presbytery. Get some big names behind you and then come back."

I'm certain now that he thought he gotten rid of me forever. But, because of what he had said, we decided to go for the biggest names we could think of—and we did.

Stanley Kresge, the founder of K-Mart, was one of the most famous Christians in Detroit, so I looked his name up in the phone book. Marilyn and I called from a public phone booth! It was amazing to me that his number was even listed, and even more astounding when Kresge himself picked up the phone. Shocked to have gotten through, Marilyn blurted out, "Billy Graham is coming to Detroit. You better help us!"

Well, Kresge did help, and so did many others. The list included Clayton Raymond of the Detroit Sunday School Convention, Joe Ninowski of Full Gospel Businessmen, Dan Ninowski of radio station WBFG, and a Baptist millionaire building contractor named Paul Johnson. Johnson was especially helpful because so many people respected him. While too busy to chair the steering committee himself, he knew someone who could. The man he had in mind was none other than Harold MacDonald at Ford Motors! He personally called Harold and challenged him to get involved.

Meanwhile, I went back to my spiritual mentor, Elizabeth MacDonald, and enlisted her aid. She joined us, urging her husband to accept the call. He not only accepted, but went on to develop the committee into a real board of directors.

Prayer or Politics?

But Billy Graham still hadn't answered our letters affirmatively. In fact, the situation was worse than that. He wrote us several nice letters saying how sorry he was he couldn't come. Somehow, God gave us the audacity to ignore the turn-downs from Graham and keep going.

I don't want to give the impression that Marilyn and I were seeing visions or hearing voices all the time! There was very little supernatural evidence that we were obeying God. Mostly we would just pray and talk with God in a conversational way, asking Him to show us the next step.

As we obeyed, God directed. In this way, one day at time, we saw the crusade beginning to take shape. Prayer and obedience were always our watchwords.

We felt our way along from one victory to the next. One day, I accidentally met the son of a former Graham Crusade board member. His dad set up meetings for Billy Graham at the Michigan State Fairgrounds back in the 1950s. He told me the Graham people wouldn't accept our invitation until a certain number of key local church leaders would unite and agree to officially invite him.

That was the clue we needed to launch another whole thrust. We organized a group of mothers into a group called "Concerned Citizens for Billy Graham." For the next two years, without any encouragement from the Graham headquarters in Minneapolis, we started circulating petitions in the congregations and neighborhoods. We urged everyone to promise their support and write letters asking for the Graham Crusade.

From time to time, newspapers or radio stations would call me to ask, "When is Billy Graham coming to Detroit?"

"I don't know—but soon" I would reply, trying to sound confident.

They persisted, "How do you know he's really coming?"

"Because the Lord told me so," I answered sincerely.

Not surprisingly, a good many folks in the media and church community alike thought our mother's campaign for Billy Graham was approaching the lunatic fringe of religion.

Finally in the third year of our letter-writing solicitation, we mysteriously had a breakthrough from Minneapolis. The Graham Association said that a crusade was possible for October, 1976, if the churches would agree to support the ten-day event with the necessary finances and volunteers for counseling, transportation and publicity.

This was the turning point. Harold MacDonald was able to line up enough churches and promises of support. The steering committee incorporated, and we had an organization.

I'll never forget how everything began to change. Professional fund-raisers and advance men began visiting almost every week from the Graham organization. This was my first experience with consultants.

The ladies were very intimidated by these brusque men in suits. Our little group of ten key women found ourselves more and more uncomfortable in the prayer and planning meetings. The tone had changed—much less prayer and much more planning!

Pretty soon, we found ourselves excused from the business meetings. We were meeting alone again just to pray, while the men took over the operations. I didn't comprehend what had happened. We had somehow lost the ball! I'm sure that if I had understood what was going on, I could have tried to keep control and remain prominent. Looking back, I'm glad I was too naive to try.

The Constant Choice: Control or Growth

You see, a real prophet doesn't seek control. Truth-telling and call-giving are enough. A real intercessor doesn't seek control either. Hearing from God is enough. If the Lord God gives you a vision for something, it is quite likely to grow beyond your ability to manage it. You will soon have to make a choice: either release the movement to others, or try to hold on and smother it to death!

This is the choice "life-givers" must make time and again in developing any Christian ministry; it's the choice between control and growth. You can try to keep power in your hands and pull all the strings, or you can let go, trust the Holy Spirit, and see a real move of God.

The choice also works the other way. Leaders with fragile egos and controlling spirits rarely start new moves unless they work with a birth-team of intercessors and prophets. Even when they start a super-church or a powerful mission, it fizzles fast unless they are humble enough to keep recruiting intercessors and prophets to call the work forward. The Bible is full of tragic stories of kings and leaders who refused to listen to God's anointed prophets.

Had Marilyn Flora, Ann Avesian and I tried to go beyond our ministries of conception and hold governing power, Billy Graham might never have come to Detroit in 1976. Thousands of souls would never have found the Savior. But by returning to our prayer closets where it all began, we were able to let the Harold MacDonalds take over and bring the impossibilities of that crusade into reality.

That was my first great lesson in spiritual warfare and the power of the unified body of Christ. We prophets exercised our faith to proclaim big plans, but God gave us the grace and humility not to try to implement them all by ourselves! Victory only comes when all the gifts work together.

Invisible for God

This is what the Lord showed me that night through my tears in the Pontiac Silverdome. He challenged me to take my place in the kingdom of God, to be content with it, and to develop it fully without looking aside to covet other offices.

Just as Moses got to see Canaan land from the top of Mount Pisgah, the Lord was permitting me to see some of the dramatic results I could have if I would take my place in a ministry of prayer and prophecy. As Moses' view from Mount Pisgah was his bittersweet reward, so my panoramic seat in "stadium heaven" was mine.

I realize now that the Lord didn't even have to let me sit there and look down on the results of my first labor, to see the baby after it was born. In fact, that was a greater reward than most intercessors ever see!

Faith, after all, is *"the evidence of things not seen"* (Hebrews 11:1). For centuries, thousands of intercessors have been crying out to God for an awakening in closed lands. Many saints have died still believing God for unanswered prayers. Prophecy and intercessory prayer ministries demand that kind of unrewarded faith. It takes a special gifting to labor behind the scenes, far from the action, trusting God to vindicate the tears.

So what joy it is when we do get to see answers to prayers! As I sat there in the Silverdome watching hundreds go forward to accept Christ, the Lord spoke clearly to me:

> *These are all the fruit of your womb. You don't need the glory or the power of the kingdom. Those things belong to Me. Your ministry is simply to pray for the harvest and speak it into existence as I command you.*
>
> *This is what I have done through you. This is the ministry I am calling you to, a ministry to conceive and nurture My end-times move among the nations. Learn how to be content in your prayer closet and work behind the scenes with leaders. Trust Me to bring the fruit in My season.*

I suddenly realized why God choose Gideon's tiny band to rout the Philistines, why the walls of Jericho fell without a fight, why Jesus was born in a manger rather than a palace. God does not share His glory. It isn't right for us to receive the recognition we crave. Seeking the spotlight is sin. By denying me fame and recognition,

God was actually keeping me from being tempted above that which I was able to handle.

God's glory is not negotiable; it is not shared with His servants. If we take any of it for ourselves, that is stealing—not just petty theft, but the kind of stealing that puts us in league with Satan. His rebellion against the Lord began because he coveted God's glory for himself.

Our flesh wants to be seen and heard. But the Holy Spirit in us shuns personal glory and leads us to magnify Christ. Only His glory is to be seen in our lives and ministries.

Smashing Spiritual Barriers

Although still just a babe in Christ, birthing the Graham Crusade brought me face-to-face with long-established barriers of religious, cultural and economic traditions. Satan had woven a dark curtain around the city of Detroit designed to keep out the light of God's love and truth. Praying that crusade into existence was a crash course in spiritual warfare.

Although I didn't fully realize what it meant, I had also discovered the calling of God on my life. Through travailing, listening prayer that resulted in anointed prophecy, I saw how I could have a part in a miraculous, creative ministry. If I could bring cities and nations to Christ, no part of my world was outside of God's control.

God wants to use us to release billions of people who are now being held captive in Satanic strongholds—whole territories, tribes and tongues which are still without a witness of the Lord Jesus Christ. Who will join us in giving birth to these souls?

The battle for end-times evangelism, revival and awakening is not just assigned to missionaries, pastors, evangelists and teachers. This work belongs just as much to us who intercede for the lost. We pray to the Lord to send laborers to gather the harvest. Intercessors and prophets are needed today as never before to sound the trumpet and call out soldiers of the cross. Even alone in her kitchen, an intercessor can have as great an impact on this world as the greatest evangelist preaching in Moscow or Beijing or Mecca.

God excludes no one from this powerful ministry. No council, synod or bishop need ordain you—and none can deny you your place at the throne of God! It is a ministry for all—not just the beautiful, educated, famous, rich and talented. The elderly, the weak and the humble are welcome in the Holy of Holies. Even bench-warmers who have been sidelined by human coaches can be first-string players in spiritual warfare. It is no wonder the Lord promised that the last shall be first and the first last.

This is the secret ministry we discovered in the Billy Graham years. In 1976, God changed the course of my life—setting me up for a worldwide ministry I never knew existed.

When the oral historian from the Billy Graham Center in Wheaton, Illinois interviewed me for their archives, she asked me to tell in one sentence how the 1976 Detroit Crusade got started. "By hearing from God one step at time, and acting out our faith," I replied simply. I think that is the formula for every great move of God—faith and obedience.

Then, as she wrapped up the interview, she asked me one last question, "What is next for Nancy Milsk?"

I wasn't ready for the question, but as I started to answer, a strange tingling sensation came over me as God revealed an inspired answer. "Calling the body of Christ together for end-times revival," I answered confidently, feeling as if my voice were almost disembodied.

I gave that answer not having a clue of how the Lord was going to do it, or even what "end-times revival" was all about. But I had learned by now that I didn't need to have all the answers to speak the mind of Christ. God would show me the next step as I presented to Him *"ears to hear"* (Mark 4:23).

Chapter 3

Women Seeking All of God

And you will seek Me and find Me,
when you search for Me with all your heart.
—Jeremiah 29:13

As I waited for God to indicate the next step on my spiritual journey, it became progressively harder to get along with my traditional church friends. I tried to relate new spiritual experiences to all the important people in my life, especially my women friends at church. I never could keep secrets. Even as a child, I loved to tell stories and announce the latest news!

In 1972, I discovered that God literally answers prayer. Tensions really heightened after that. Before then, the strivers and doubters in our group only debated Bible verses with me. Now they had to argue against miracles as well!

I would see a supernatural answer to prayer and couldn't help but bubble over with testimony. My exclamations that "Jesus is real!" or "Christ still heals today!" were met first with polite put-downs, then "not-again" stares, and finally with outright hostility. I didn't share to provoke negative responses, but I got them anyway.

My witnessing was taken as judgmentalism by the proud churchwomen of our congregation. Most of them were raised in religious homes, but they weren't having faith experiences like these—nor did they particularly welcome them!

You Talk Too Much!

One day, a girlfriend bluntly summed up what I suppose a lot of people had been thinking. "You're too loud!" she accused, "Have you ever thought of becoming a Baptist?"

Another exasperated friend lost it and blurted out, "You know, Nancy, you talk too much!"

"I know," I replied, "but I'm supposed to be a big talker! God has called me to be His mouthpiece." I tried to explain my experience of being called to be a prophet from Jeremiah 1:5, but it was like trying to talk over a ten-foot stone wall. There was simply no place in our church for the voice of God to interrupt the program.

Life on the Cutting Edge

Dutifully, I managed to remain a faithful member for nearly four years, keeping one foot in each world. With all my heart, I wanted to bring the two together. I'd meet for tea with the nice, "together" Christians on one day, then go out the next to meet with women on the growing edge.

Often, this meant sitting teary-eyed at a kitchen table, praying with some broken-hearted housewife who hadn't been to church for months, sometimes years. As in Christ's parable of the Pharisee and the publican, I kept finding that it was usually the "wrong kind of people" who humbly sought God! Most often, they were messed-up sinners, women whose lives were not in order.

For some strange reason, these women were also the ones who didn't eat their salads with the right fork or know how to keep a dinner napkin balanced on their knees! I had a hard time bringing them to my church where our brand of social Christianity made them so very uncomfortable.

Beyond Cultural Christianity

I didn't know it, but my double life was transforming me into a hardened "gospel groupie." Soon, wherever there was lively daytime Bible study, I was there. Christ became so real that I couldn't stay away from His people. I was hooked! I needed the fellowship and nurture that wasn't available in tradition-bound churches.

At first, Charles thought my group attendance was just a fad. "Be sure to tell me when you move out of our house and start living at church," he kidded one night.

The more God showed me, the more I wanted. Revelation is progressive, just as Christ promised in John 14:21. He rewards obedient hearts and promises to manifest Himself to them in a special way. The more you obey, the more you receive!

I soon found out that I wasn't the only one with an insatiable hunger for God. There were other women like me in our subdivision. They were also unashamedly meeting to read their Bibles and search for intimacy with Him. All had one goal: we wanted our faith to be real in our everyday lives as homemakers, mothers and wives.

With Christ in the Ladies Room

That was what made Elizabeth MacDonald's testimony so powerful to me and many others. She was a vibrant, totally alive woman who was successfully applying Christian ideas to her marriage and family. She had a jump on the rest of us. Elizabeth was older. When she prefaced advice with the phrase, "I've been 36 years in the Lord," we sat up and listened. Here was a successful woman who had walked with God since before I was born.

Here was an obvious example of *"Let the older women teach the younger"* (Titus 2:4). She had more authority in our circles than Billy Graham, Charleston Heston and Dr. Spock combined!

Discovering God's Word

There was never any question that we would take the Bible literally in our study. Although we included just about every denomination, there was an unwritten rule: we didn't let our traditions or human reasoning reduce the simple impact of Scripture.

It was God's holy Word. We studied the pure Bible in a frankly devotional way, with hearts eager to obey it. We questioned everything that was taught or written about the Word in our search for truth. Any new idea that was introduced to the group was checked against Scripture.

Once, somebody quoted the old saw, "God helps those who help themselves," as if it were biblical.

"Where is that in the Bible?" I asked innocently, thinking that it must be in there. We all looked, finally realizing that it wasn't! Embarrassed, I vowed to always have scriptural proof for anything I believed.

I'm convinced the reason we experienced such a powerful presence of God in our groups was this total dependence on God's Word coupled with childlike faith. It also kept us from error. I would sometimes hear of others doing strange or silly things, but since we questioned anything not in the Bible, we never had those kinds of problems.

Faith in the Neighborhood

Soon, almost all my daytime hours were devoted to "coffee-klatching" with other women. The testimony of my new born-again experience attracted other seekers like honey draws bees. I became a connecting link.

It was easy to network from one group to the next. I found myself becoming like the Christians in Acts, which says they went *"breaking bread from house to house ...with gladness and simplicity of heart"* (Acts 2:46).

Ellen Smith was one of several seekers I found in those days among my own neighbors. Divorced and alone, she was desperately trying to raise two tiny preschoolers without a regular income. Circumstances made her substitute faith for finances.

Ellen was the first person I met who even trusted God for parking spaces. Each desperate new situation drove her deeper into the hands of the living Lord. The God she knew through faith was more tangible than the physical world. He healed without medicine and provided milk and eggs in answer to prayer.

An Army brat in World War II, I was raised by a father who left nothing to chance. He was a colonel, a civil engineer who selected a practical woman for a wife. A no-nonsense school teacher, Mom taught me to believe that "God helps those who help themselves." (It was the cornerstone of their religion and why I must have believed it was actually in the Bible!)

My parents made no provision for divine providence to rescue us from trials or sickness. Life was harsh. Sickness and shortages were certain realities. Everyone worked hard, planned for every bit of bad luck, and washed out their own underwear every night! So while I was raised by God-fearing parents, I certainly was never taught to exercise or stretch my faith for miracles!

Will God Pay the Grocery Bills?

One day I arrived early for our regular Bible study. Ellen was still dressing. "Make yourself comfortable," she called out cheerfully from the bedroom.

I casually opened the refrigerator to get out the coffee and cream for the meeting—that's where Ellen always kept them—but there was no Hills Brothers in sight. In fact the shelves were nearly empty. Nothing is as empty as an empty refrigerator!

"How can she feed the kids?" I asked myself. Curiously I peeked around, trying to figure out how I would put something together for dinner if I were in her shoes. All her cupboards and cabinets were equally bare. There simply wasn't enough food left for the kids that night —and this was only the middle of the month! Even if her child support check came on time, I figured quickly it would still be two weeks before she had any cash.

I realized there was no way Ellen ever had enough to live on. Trying to imagine how we would survive without Chuck's paycheck, I wondered where she got the new faith every morning to keep going like this. Ellen was literally trusting God for survival from day to day!

Not mentioning the missing coffee, I attempted to act naturally as the other girls arrived. We gathered our little group around the kitchen table for Bible study. Ellen shared her need for prayer for her financial situation. It was the same request she always gave, but it came without a hint of despair.

Was she putting us on? I wondered if anyone else at the table shared my secret knowledge. She couldn't afford sugar for the coffee, let alone the coffee!

How could she be so calm? There were no food banks then in our well-to-do Jewish neighborhood. (Secondhand canned goods were for the inner-city poor—not us!) Yet Ellen was obviously destitute.

I thought of the words from the Lord's prayer, *"Give us this day our daily bread"* (Matthew 6:11). Those were mere words to me before that day. Here was someone who really had to believe God for her daily bread!

God worked on my heart as I walked home. I had to help. In my kitchen, I soon found myself filling a grocery bag. Returning to her place, I found that God was moving in other hearts, too. Someone else had already been there. On the doorstep was a bag of groceries left anonymously by another merciful soul. Quietly setting my bag down alongside the other, I backed away, marveling at the miracle of God's provision.

The Spirit had worked simultaneously in the hearts of His servants without human organization. Professional charity is seldom needed when God's people are in harmony with each other and the Spirit.

Bitter Advice

Still amazed, the next Tuesday I couldn't wait to share this testimony with my church sisters. "Guess what, you guys!" I said as excited as a child with a new toy. "My neighbor didn't have any food left, and we just prayed, and there were groceries on the doorstep. God answers prayer! Isn't He wonderful?"

"Yes, that's good," said one matron, dryly dismissing my testimony, "but you better tell her to go get a job!"

Soon after, Ellen had a terrible gallstone attack. Not knowing what to do, several of us prayed for healing. I drove her to the emergency room at Beaumont Hospital.

When the doctor examined her, the pain was gone. He announced that there was nothing wrong. "You can take her home," he smiled.

"What about her gallstones?" I asked.

Turning and walking away, he called back without looking me in the eye, "There are no stones."

Again, I had a great testimony to share, this time about God's healing power. I saw the faces of the group stubbornly harden as I detailed the events. No one wanted to give God the glory for this second miracle—or even acknowledge His intervention in the natural world.

"Well," one lady finally snipped, "my family had gallstones for years. They always came back and aren't healed by prayer. Believe me, she needs surgery. You better tell her to get ready for the next attack!"

I was speechless at such determined unbelief, but relieved to drop the subject. I felt ashamed and guilty, not knowing yet that God didn't need me to defend His honor from scoffers. How could such skepticism come from Christians? I had no way to answer or combat it.

Different Levels of Faith

Soon after that, I decided to make a break. I was reading the story of the great apostles Paul and Barnabas in Acts 15:36-41. Here were two fine missionaries who had a serious difference of opinion and faith levels. I realized that even Paul didn't have the faith to believe that Mark would endure. But Barnabas did; he was all for giving Mark another chance.

No doubt both men were serving the Lord to the best of their abilities and successfully doing the work of

God. Even so, they realized they had to part. There is no indication in this passage that they broke fellowship or divided the body of Christ.

Remember, Paul was always a champion of unity, pleading that we all *"speak the same thing"* and *"be perfectly joined together in the same mind and in the same judgment"* (1 Corinthians 1:10). Nevertheless, he realized they couldn't go on working together with such different faith levels.

As I read this passage, the Lord applied it to my home church situation. I didn't have to feel guilty about leaving my traditional church in order to grow and obey Him. Sometimes God calls you to stay, but not always. I realized I could no longer work with their faith level.

The ladies in my church were content to go on being doubting Thomases even after the Lord had offered to let them touch the nail prints in His hand! They had reached a faith-plateau on which they were settled.

Some folks draw a line in their lives. God is not allowed to go beyond that point. But not me. I sensed the Lord calling me higher. There would be no such lines in my life. Sometimes, like Abram in Ur, it becomes necessary to leave your people and homeland. I had to let God out of the "faith box" my church had made for Him, even if it meant leaving behind friends I loved.

I had to find new friends who would not cage God. I needed people who were unafraid to take my hand and say, "Come on, let's go deeper in obedience. Let's explore the passionate heart of Jesus together."

What about My Family?

My only remaining worry was over Charles and the kids. Our traditional church was the only spiritual home they knew. They didn't have a clue what was happening in my spirit. I didn't know how to explain the changes to my family. Chuck had never been to one of our women's prayer groups—and I'm sure he would have felt like he had accidentally walked into the ladies room if he did!

I was mortally afraid to tell him how deeply into my heart this born-again conversion was going, afraid he would get upset and think I had gone overboard. It wasn't that Chuck was irreligious. We had worked all our married life to be respectable! To please me, he always went along to church and Sunday school. It was good for business and the socially correct thing in our circles. Everyone belonged to some kind of church or synagogue.

How was I going to share my new faith which had now gone so far beyond nominal church membership? What would happen to my family if I dropped out of church to meet informally in houses? For hours and days I worried. Yet God kept calling me out like Abraham.

God Speaks from Jeremiah

My very first call to ministry came soon after my conversion.

It was snowing again, a bitterly cold February day. The skies were battleship gray, the way they get for weeks at a time in Great Lakes winters. I had been invited to one of the oldest, most-respected Presbyterian churches in Birmingham. It was a well-established congregation that met in a lovely stone building, so beautiful it could have come right off a calendar page.

The meetings was interdenominational. Much later, it would become known as "the" interfaith renewal group for Birmingham. But then, it was still without a label, as were most groups in the move of God back then.

My husband had just bought me a brand new car. I waited for the good feeling to come from driving this beautiful Oldsmobile Supreme. It was a rich butterscotch color with real leather seats, but somehow the luxury didn't have the effect I expected. My kids, the house, the car and all the nice things that Charles' financial success brought me were still not filling the void in my life. Something spiritual was yet missing, a purpose in life beyond my salvation.

Betty Friedan's *Feminine Mystique* had spawned hundreds of books for women that told us to dare to be all we could be! Even though I had just found Christ as Savior, I prayed in frustration as I drove. "What is my purpose in life, Lord? Is this all there is?" I cried and complained. "Where do I fit in Your grand plan? Why did I go to college and get my degree—and then grad school?"

I parked the car. Inside, I joined the others already meeting in a large Sunday-school room. To this day, I can't remember anything about the program or the speaker. But I can never forget the text. It was Jeremiah 1:5-10, and I still have it underlined in my old Bible. Certain phrases popped out as a direct answer to my heart's cry in the car for vocational purpose.

Till the End of Time

I read the text over and over:

> *Before I formed you in the womb I knew you...and I ordained you a prophet to the nations...Do not be afraid of their faces...I have put My words in your mouth...I have set you over the nations and over the kingdoms.* (Jeremiah 1:5, 8-10)

The room and everyone in it faded away. Suddenly I saw myself in Jeremiah's role. I heard the Lord saying:

Nancy, My call is upon you as it was on Jeremiah. You are to be a mouthpiece for Me to your generation and to the nations. You will have an international ministry from Me.

Do not be afraid. You can speak for Me. You're not too young. I have called you as Mine. Speak for Me.

The meeting had ended. Yet bluebirds were singing in my heart and fireworks exploding in my spirit. Most of the people had already left, but I was too enthralled by the text to move from my seat. It was as if the angel of the Lord had paralyzed me.

Finally, I got up and interrupted the knot of people that had stayed behind to talk at the altar. "Can you believe it?" I asked. "God says this is for me! I am to speak what He commands. He is sending me to the nations!"

Choosing not to notice the strange looks I was getting, I went back and worshipped the Lord in private ecstasy until the room suddenly went dark. "We're leaving now," I heard a stern voice say. "We're turning out the lights. You have to go."

In the hallway, I opened my Bible one last time and pointed to the text. "That's me!" I said to the stern man. "Can you believe this? God says this text is for me."

"You have to go," was all the man said. His tone was one of rejection and isolation. To this day, he probably still thinks I was just another crazy charismatic who wandered into the meeting.

That was the first defining moment of my ministry, yet I had never felt more humanly alone in my life—or so close to God. At last, I had found my personal purpose.

Here was my calling in the body of Christ. I was being set aside, special to God, a mouthpiece for the Lord!

As I walked out of the church into the cold air, all I could do was repeat the words of Jeremiah's commission over and over. *"Do not be afraid of their faces...I have put my words in your mouth."*

Guideposts

In 1970, I hadn't discovered Christian bookstores or Christian magazines yet. Those were the days before Christian broadcasting networks. There was still no national 700 Club, PTL, TBN or the many radio and TV ministries we have today!

Yet something was happening to us women. God was moving in our lives. I wondered if we were really becoming religious fanatics like some of our friends thought. Were we going overboard, crazy for God? People couldn't understand us, and we couldn't understand ourselves.

Then one day at my mother's house, I found a little magazine called *Guideposts*. It had been there all along. Mom had been getting it for years, but I'd never flipped it open. But my new interest in a personal, living God caused me to look at the magazine in a whole new way.

The articles told of ordinary people who were discovering God in the midst of ordinary living. These were not articles about religious professionals by preachers and missionaries. *Guideposts* was about real people, just like my friends and me. God was talking to them, appearing to them, and encouraging them through everyday events. Sometimes they met God in disaster, but more often in common occurrences, such as baking cookies or finding a long-lost card. This rang true in my spirit.

Guideposts become a touch point for me in the early days of my spiritual journey. While it didn't go deep into

Bible teachings or explain spiritual gifts, it reassured us that we could encounter God at our kitchen tables or while waiting in the dentist's chair.

I reasoned that if God could speak to those people, He could speak to me, too. If He was present in the events of their lives, then He was present in the events of mine. I wasn't going crazy after all!

Women all across the United States were experiencing the same kinds of feelings that had driven my search for God. I wasn't alone anymore. Later I would realize there were millions of us, both men and women, who were finding God in the sacraments of everyday life rather than formal religion.

Journaling My Journey with Jesus

I began to understand that I was really on a quest for the Lord when a friend named Avonale Slagle invited me to an all-day workshop on spiritual journaling. It was sponsored by a local chapter of the Christian Women's Club in Farmington.

Starting a diary of my spiritual journey made me aware for the first time that my search for God was not really accidental, although it seemed to be taking place in random, unorganized ways. Writing my spiritual journal showed me that God had been weaving a pattern —in my life all along. I realized that I was on a voyage of discovery. God was calling me closer to Himself even though I didn't know how to find the next door—or what it would be like once I opened it!

Two other things happened in my journaling group, one pleasant and one not so pleasant. Both led me to the same place, to Mother Beall and the Bethesda Missionary Armory, deep in the inner city of Detroit.

Struggling with Baptism

The pleasant event was finding a way to enter into water baptism. I couldn't remember ever having been baptized. Whenever the subject came up, I always felt a tugging in my heart. The Holy Spirit was compelling me to follow the Lord into the baptismal waters. I really wanted to obey Christ in this matter, although no one ever sat down and taught me on the subject.

I was terrified to tell Charles about this or talk to my pastor. What would people think at church if I asked to be baptized? Wouldn't it seem hypocritical at my age? It just wasn't done in our denomination. I couldn't recall ever seeing an adult baptized. That was something that "holy rollers" and other "crazies" did. I didn't dare ask for it in my church.

When the subject came up again in my journaling group, several ladies deftly quoted the Scriptures about baptism. "Well," I convinced myself, "here's something else I need!" Although I was sure I wanted to be baptized as Christ was, I was still embarrassed about how, when and where.

Avonale knew my fears of talking with Charles about this kind of thing. I thought of asking the folks at Highland Park Baptist, but I had seen big wading boots hanging in the back of their baptistry—and I was afraid that I might have to wear them! "I know just who you need," giggled Avonale in a teasing whisper. "She's fabulous for you!"

"Who?" I asked in the same conspiratorial whisper.

"Mother Beall!" she exclaimed triumphantly.

Avonale must have seen the wonder in my eyes. Was I supposed to know her?

"Who's Mother Beall?" I begged.

"Don't worry. I'll take you. It'll be our secret," she assured me. "You won't have to tell Charles or your friends or anyone at church! I'll help you get baptized. We'll go next Thursday."

Discovering Yet Another Baptism

The unpleasant part of the journaling group grew from my testimony about Ellen's miracle answers to prayer. I was still bubbling over with the joy of her healing and the other healings that were becoming a routine part of our house fellowships.

As I read the Gospels, healing always seemed to be a part of our Lord's ministry. I took it for granted that Christ would heal now, just as He did then! But when I began to praise the Lord and tell the story of how God answered our prayers, I faced an avalanche of criticism from my fellow journalists.

I could hardly speak as several of the women in the group ganged up on me, insisting that healing wasn't for today. They had chapter and verse to prove their position. Not only didn't God heal, they scolded, but all other supernatural evidences of His power ended in the book of Acts.

They especially attacked something called the baptism in the Holy Spirit and the "tongues movement." These were new phrases to me. I didn't even know there was a "tongues movement," but if somebody else also believed in healing and miracles, I was curious!

Having already seen God heal, I knew that was real for today. And if so, maybe the other things that happened in the book of Acts were real as well!

After the meeting, I was almost in tears. Avonale just smiled her secret smile at me. "Why was healing so wrong?" I asked. "Why couldn't God choose to reveal Himself today in miracles?

"Of course He can," said Avonale confidently. "Don't let them get you down."

"And what is the baptism in the Holy Spirit?" I asked, sensing that Avonale knew something that I didn't.

"Don't worry about that, my dear," she said with a twinkle in her eye. "Mother Beall can answer your questions about both baptisms. About everything. I think today has been a divine appointment for you. You're ready for some real discipling and teaching. We've got to get you established that's all!"

A Glass of the Holy Spirit

However, as it happened, I didn't need to wait to see Mother Beall to learn about the Holy Spirit. One day soon after, I sat all alone at our kitchen table listening to a local Christian radio station. The kids were still at school. A speaker came on the air, preaching from the book of Acts. His subject was the baptism in the Holy Spirit!

He spoke on Acts 2:4, *"And they were all filled with the Holy Spirit and began to speak with other tongues, as the Spirit gave them utterance."* He explained that this filling was the exact same power to witness that the Lord promised in Acts 1:8. I didn't need any more definition.

The brother argued that it was no harder to receive the baptism of the Spirit than drinking a glass of water. You just open your mouth, and another language comes out!

I opened my mouth, but nothing came out. As the broadcast ended, I continued to sit at my table, opening my mouth. "Lord," I cried aloud, "I want the power you promised to be a witness for you!" Still nothing.

Then I had an idea. Why not follow directions? I went over to the sink and grabbed an empty glass from the drying rack. Filling it with water, I took a drink. "It's just like drinking a glass of water," I repeated.

I opened my mouth and out came a series of monosyllables. It sounded like baby talk to me. Soon streams of bizarre sounds were coming out rhythmically. It was strange—certainly not English. But was it really the baptism in the Holy Spirit? I hoped so. Something had happened. I guessed I would find out for sure on Thursday at Mother Beall's.

Chapter 4

First Encounters with the Move of God

Therefore we were buried with Him through baptism into death, that just as Christ was raised from the dead by the glory of the Father, even so we also should walk in newness of life.
—Romans 6:4

Bethesda Missionary Armory was appropriately named. The sprawling brick fortress was an East Detroit landmark. Its ramparts overlooked decaying neighborhoods once filled with hard-working European immigrants —folks who supplied muscle for Detroit's automotive assembly lines.

Now, the Armory and the woman who built it were ending an era of ministry. White-flight panic changed whole communities. The building was eventually purchased by a thriving black congregation which went in a new direction.

But before that, curious carloads of suburban sophisticates began showing up on the steps of Bethesda. Among them was my friend Avonale. The attraction was Mother Beall. She had built the block-long structure with four decades of faith. Before her physical death, she

69

had one last task: to plant the seeds of a new move of God in our hearts.

The Genius of Metro-wide Ministry

This lighthouse at Van Dyke and Nevada was still carrying on the big metro ministry that made it famous. At evening rallies, visiting celebrities like Corrie Ten Boom and Nicky Cruz continued to fill the 2,000-seat auditorium.

Bethesda was a remarkable institution that combined church, Bible institute and youth center into a Christian temple that never seemed to close. It began during World War II as a 24-hour Christian servicemen's center. Mom Beall loved to retell the old stories of sailors who came to the center. They were born-again, water-baptized, filled with the Spirit, and commissioned to take the Gospel overseas—all during one 48-hour shore leave!

It was an old fashioned deliverance temple, born in the midst of an earlier revival. During the so-called "latter-rain movement," Bethesda was constructed by mysterious volunteers who appeared at just the right stage when needed to plaster, plumb or wire! In a tough union town like Detroit, this was a double miracle.

Missionaries with various spiritual gifts came through over the years to minister. This made the Armory a spiritual treasury for greater Detroit.

Handmaiden to it all, Mother Beall presided over a citywide outreach with awesome spiritual authority. As a young wife, she had left her beloved Methodist church to direct the daring new inner-city mission with her husband, Harry. When I first met her, she was in her eighties.

Avonale dragged me to Bethel with the sure-footed zeal of Andrew bringing Simon to Christ. "You need to be rooted and grounded," she insisted, certain I would get much more than just the water baptism I sought.

Believer's Baptism and the Holy Spirit

I'd never seen a Missionary Armory before, but as we pulled up it seemed greater to me than any of the great cathedrals in Europe. Inside, I felt the sense of sacred space increase as we walked into the assistant pastor's office.

"Look," I said breathlessly as we sat down, "I've got to get baptized in water. No one can do it on a weekday. Could you baptize me?"

"Yes," the pastor replied, accepting my urgency as if it were perfectly normal, "there is another candidate in the Thursday morning class who also wants baptism. You can take instruction together. We'll fill the pool and do it right after chapel."

Good, I thought to myself, that will give me enough time afterwards to have my hair done before I get home so Charles won't even know I was baptized. (Things were moving so fast that I still hadn't told Charles of my decision to leave our church! What would he think of me going to the inner city for baptism?)

So it was all set. Avonale led me into the chapel where Mother Beall was already teaching 200 disciples from a wheelchair. There was an aura about her I could not understand. She radiated God's glory and power. She spoke easily for Him, just as Elizabeth MacDonald had. "How can I be like that?" I wondered.

Now I was certain Avonale was right. Exposure to this woman would take me deeper into the Lord. So for the next three years, I absorbed the teachings and lifestyle of Mother Beall. She became my principal mentor.

Identified with Christ at Last!

A former missionary to Africa named Paul Stern celebrated my baptism. As I reached out to greet him, my whole hand just disappeared into his enormous fingers! He made me feel like I was six years old again, talking with my earthly father. It felt good to entrust my baptism to this man.

Feeling faint, I walked into the huge theater that served as Bethesda's sanctuary. All across the front was the longest altar rail I'd ever seen, with 15 to 20 feet of empty space cleared in front of it for ministry.

On the huge stage was a platform, the pulpit and a big choir loft. High above the loft, the baptistry was built dramatically into the wall. It looked like a picture frame, just big enough to display one baptism at a time.

By now I had met with Avonale's study group, going through all the Scriptures about baptism. They believed that baptism was not just symbolic theater, but had real spiritual significance.

Slipping into a long white robe, I prepared for God to do something new in me as I identified with Christ's death and resurrection. I longed for this sacred moment of unity with Christ!

As I entered the cold water from stage left, the 2,000 empty seats emphasized how private this step was. But that made it all the more personal and meaningful to me.

Paul and a small group of witnesses took their time reading the Scriptures and exhorting me. I confessed my faith in the Lord, the icy waters forgotten. As Paul took me in his huge hands, I looked up at him and said, "I think I have the Holy Spirit, but I'm not sure."

"Nancy," he replied, "all the angels in heaven have been waiting for this day—let it rip!" And with that, he lowered me backwards into the cold wetness. His strength amazed me. I felt like a rag doll in his hands.

As I came up out of the waters, I was baptized afresh with the Holy Spirit. I began praising the Lord in the most beautiful supernatural language I had ever heard. These were not like the stuttering monosyllables at my kitchen table. Instead I spoke in a powerful cadence. The echoes of a glorious heavenly language pierced the farthest corner of that darkened hall.

In fact, the poetry of that praise was so real that I almost felt that the Holy Spirit was singing through me. God doesn't want to fill us just once. Holy Spirit baptism is a multiple event that goes on and on. We must remain open to receiving many baptisms as we make our spiritual journeys.

Years of Tears

So began what I call my years of tears. At Bethesda, every Scripture and every lesson seemed to show me areas where I needed repentance and amendment in my life. Godly sorrow brought weeping as I saw how far from God's ways were my ways.

I felt like an onion being peeled one layer at a time as I entered into sanctification. Christ was calling me deeper and deeper. Every week we drove to East Detroit through the concrete canyons of the Lodge and Davidson Freeways.

Then I would sit in the chapel under Mother Beall, usually in the third or fourth row. Everything she said from that platform hit my spirit like a wrecking ball. Prophecy was part of nearly every service.

Although we worshipped and prayed, Thursday chapel was like no other church service I had ever attended. It was like having an appointment with the living God. Many of her prophecies were intensely personal.

Speaking directly to me, her personal challenge was almost always the same maddening cry, *"Come out, come out from among them. Don't cling to the world!"* What did I need to come out from?

One day I asked, "Where should I go?"

Mother Beall had no denomination or organization for me to join. Startled, she looked at me as if I should have already known the answer. "Into Christ, of course!" she said, "Where else?"

Irresistible to God

Through the months that followed, it was as if Christ were stripping and cleaning me with a wire brush. Bethesda was my sanctuary and seminary, a place of ever-deepening commitment to personal holiness.

I was being called to lay aside every weight, every idol and every sin. I was learning how to be attractive and irresistible to God through holiness. It is Christ who does this, who makes us beautiful to God through His holiness.

God asked for my diplomas, my honors, my career hopes, my books—even the writings of famous teachers and evangelists. I surrendered them. He put His holy finger on anything I kept between Him and me, whether secular or religious. I learned that Christ is a consuming fire, a jealous God who permits neither disloyalty nor infidelity from His servants.

I was not allowed to even covet another's anointing. One day a friend from Highland Park Baptist called to invite me to speak at a women's group nearby. Elizabeth MacDonald had been invited, but couldn't go. This was my first invitation to speak formally, and I eagerly accepted.

The Lord blessed with a special evangelistic anointing. I came back thankful that God had allowed me to give my first invitation and to lead a woman to Christ. I felt like Peter on the Mount of Transfiguration. It was good to be used of God in the supernatural realm. I was impatient for more of it.

I wanted to stay there and built a tent! I was ready to go on the road full-time as an evangelist for Christ! I rushed to the altar at Bethesda and fell on my face before the Lord. "Give me souls!" I wept. "Let me lay in the stream of your Holy Spirit and flow through me!"

Stewing Our Gifts

But heaven did not respond. God had not commissioned me to go anywhere yet, especially as an evangelist. Instead, I felt Him telling me to sit still, to just wait. This is normal in God's economy. He is not hyperactive like we are.

Waiting on God is a vital part of any ministry. There's usually a time of enforced expectancy and preparation after a vision from the Lord. You have to wait for your gift to be developed. You have to be pregnant and carry it to term before you can bring it forth.

Waiting time is not wasted time. It gives you space to work the new gift into your own spirit, to stir it up as Paul urged Timothy, to be humble before it. If you don't "stew" your spiritual gifts long enough, you won't have wisdom to use them correctly.

Since we will be held accountable for every teaching and every word we speak in this life, we must welcome waiting times. Anyone who wants to be truly used of God has to turn off the television and the radio. We must relearn the quiet-time arts to hear God.

The Bible has a lot to say about waiting on Him. The Bethesda years gave me time to practice this important work. Before and after each ministerial action, the Lord was teaching me to spend hours on my knees.

We need to welcome times of stillness rather than resist them. *"Wait on the Lord; Be of good courage. And He shall strengthen your heart; Wait, I say, on the Lord!"* (Psalm 27:14).

Breaking Racial Pride

Bethesda also mobilized me for cross-cultural missionary service. For the first time, I learned to reach out in love to different nationalities.

In chapel there were *babushka* grandmas from Poland and the Ukraine, Hispanics from Puerto Rico and Mexico, Jews and Afro-Americans. I saw the body of Christ for the first time as Paul had described, with neither Jew nor Greek, male or female, slave or free.

I learned that economic status and gender are irrelevant, too, but the lesson didn't come easy. Detroit is a racist, segregated city, and I was very much a product of my environment.

Our group of white socialites from Birmingham always sat together if we could. It was scary to go down into the city, especially after the King riots. One day we were late, and I wasn't able to sit with my friends. I ended up with black women on both sides of me.

Then Mother Beall announced we were going to have a footwashing service. I'd never heard of footwashing except in the Bible, and here I sat surrounded by Africans. Would I have to wash their feet? Would I have to let them wash mine? I looked for some way out, but there was no escape.

Well, something in me broke loose. A racial pride that I had denied was suddenly very alive in me. Washing black feet and having black hands wash my white feet tore down a strong wall in my life. It released a new burden in me for Afro-Americans.

Later, I would minister in many black congregations here and overseas. That footwashing opened a window that made it possible for me to love Africans in a new way. In the twinkling of an eye, black became beautiful to me.

Modern-day Mentors

Footwashing wasn't the only new practice I learned at Bethesda. I was surrounded by saintly older women in the Lord who took the time to pour themselves into me. Suddenly, I had a whole team of spiritual mentors in my life. I was like a sponge absorbing all kinds of ministries. The spiritual mothers of Bethesda operated routinely in discernment, deliverance, healing, prophecy and intercession. These ministries, most of which I'd never seen before, were everyday occurrences to them.

Pat Gruitt, Mother Beall's daughter, was the first person I ever saw travail in prayer. Her tears were real as she groaned and cried out, giving spiritual birth. I also learned about fasting, persistence, seed faith, and vow-making—prayer dimensions I never knew existed.

Paula and Reuben Aguas practically lived in the Armory, much as old Anna and Simeon lived in the temple. They were the first messianic Jews I ever met. We lived in a largely Jewish community for years, and I couldn't believe my eyes at meeting my first "Jews for Jesus!"

Paula had miraculously survived the Warsaw ghetto, escaping the holocaust. She frequently received a word of knowledge or wisdom from the Lord. And Paula loved in practical, New Testament ways. When my father-in-law died, they appeared at our door with a covered dish. But it was not just the Aguas. Such care-giving and visiting were a matter-of-fact part of the compassion ministries at Bethesda.

Established in the Word

As much as I wanted to come to Mother Beall's catechism class, there were two major barriers. First, it met weekly for a year. Also, it was in the inner city at night.

The greatest investor in my spiritual life was Avonale. Just as Priscilla and Aquila took Paul under their wings, Avonale made me her personal discipleship project. Avonale sensed that I had grown as much as I could in our Birmingham groups. Without someone to hold me accountable I would remain a spiritual baby. "Nancy," she dared, "if I went with you every week, would you sign up for class and get really discipled in the Word?"

"Sure," I said, realizing that if she was willing to escort me, I no longer had any excuse.

So we began together. Avonale met me at Northland Mall on Thursdays at 6:00 PM. I parked and rode in with her every week. She repeated class for my sake, and I received solid training. Our driving time was used for discussion and applications to my life.

At the end of the year, Charles was so impressed that he came down for our closing banquet and graduation. In this "grounding meeting," Mother Beall and the elders laid hands on each of us and spoke a personal blessing. "Nancy, the Lord has a word for you," said Mother Beall. ***"You are to set the captives free!"***

Charles Gives His Blessing

"What does that mean—set the captives free?" asked Charles when I sat back down with him. I knew he was really asking, "Well, what's next?"

"All I know is that God has called me to bring in end-times revival," I answered. I didn't want to admit to Charles how confused and undirected I really was. Sure, I was trained in the Word and ready to move out, but I really didn't know my next assignment!

"Maybe I'm supposed to stay here and learn more, or maybe Bethesda will have a place for me to minister," I said, "but I know one thing—I am called to ministry." There it was. I had blurted it out.

Charles nodded quietly. I knew then for the first time I had his consent and blessing. During this time he had stood on the sidelines, watching every move I made. While bemused by my years of church-hopping and group-attending, Charles had been more wonderful about my new lifestyle and schedule than I'd ever dreamed. My fears were groundless. He was really being supportive and patient as I explored my vocation.

We never talked about the home church which I had once nagged him into making the center of our religious lives. Instead of the spiritual crisis I had feared when we left, Chuck and the family absorbed my new faith quickly and easily.

The Kids Find Christ

As I was faithful to Christ, the Holy Spirit just brought my children along without a lot of bumps in the road. They went to vacation Bible schools and summer camps with the Baptists, where they were all born again, and to Sunday school and youth meetings at Bethesda, where they were all baptized in the Holy Spirit!

The Lord imparted life to us from many sources in the greater Detroit Christian community rather than one local congregation. I began to see the whole body of Christ in Detroit as much larger and richer than any of its local congregations.

One day I opened a letter from the secretary at our old church. It was a note asking if we wanted to remain on the church roll. I handed it to Charles wordlessly.

"I guess you've made your decision," he said, with teasing eyes hiding his seriousness. "You can't go back to playing church, can you? You're on a mission from God!"

Nearly three years had passed since I discovered Bethesda. I was beginning to think that God wanted us to settle down again in one local congregation, perhaps at Bethesda. I even began to apply for an advanced ministries course there, but then God interrupted my plans.

Called in the Bathtub!

The bathroom filled with steam as I poured my favorite bubble bath into the scalding water. I loved a good soak. The house was still, and I needed time to think. I decided to use this quiet spell to pray in the bathtub.

Holding up my book to keep it dry, I slipped into the water and started to read about the history of revival.

A voice whispered, *"I want you to lead revival."*

Thinking that I must have read the words, I looked at the page for a minute and spoke to myself, "It doesn't say that here!"

The voice repeated, *"I want you to lead revival."* It was the Lord. God was in the bathroom with me!

"What are you doing, God?" I cried in frustration, sinking deeper into the suds as chills ran down my neck and spine. "You've called me to set the captives free, to be a leader, but I don't know how to lead revival! It all seems so unformed to me. I need something concrete."

Suddenly I felt an urge to blow like a battle trumpet. I knew it was the Holy Spirit. Fearfully, I raised my hands to my mouth and tried. I made a tentative noise that came out sounding like a sick foghorn.

Joel 2:1 came to mind, *"Blow the trumpet in Zion, and sound an alarm in My holy mountain. Let all the inhabitants of the land tremble; for the day of the Lord is coming, for it is at hand."*

God spoke to my spirit, ***"Nancy, you are to be a trumpet in Zion. Blow the warning loud and clear. These are the end times. Your mouth is to be used to bring revival to My people."***

I cupped my hands to my mouth again. This time I blew a crystal clear note without the help of an instrument. It was miraculous. I was a human bugle!

God was calling me. He would help me blow the war cry notes that would call His people. God spoke again:

> *I have called you to go to rebellious houses. Now is the time to bring renewal to people who will listen and not run from Me. Call the body together to function in unity. Take down the walls that divide the body through intercession and waiting upon Me.*

Twice the Lord returned with the same message. Since then, it has been repeatedly confirmed by others.

Later, as I meditated on this call, God led me to read Joshua 1:16, *"All that you command us we will do, and wherever you send us we will go."* He was showing me through this text what my answer to this call should be.

"Lord," I surrendered. "I'll go where you send me and do what you tell me!" So the call and the obedience issue were settled in my mind. Only the "how-to" nagged at me. I was still a prophet without a king.

With more than a little fear, I finally dared to make an appointment to share my new vocation with a pastor friend. I explained that God had told me I would be a prophet for end-times revival. The pastor raised his eyebrows slightly, but at least he didn't argue with me or suggest that I might be having delusions. (Many clergy would have!) Instead, he gently asked a simple but devastating question, "Well, do signs follow?"

"What signs?" I asked back in dismay, already knowing the answer to my question. I felt color coming climbing up my cheeks. That was the one question for which I had no answer.

My confidence was instantly devastated. I felt like crawling out of the room on my hands and knees. Mumbling a nonsense answer, I escaped as quickly as I could in confused shame. It was as if I had been shot in the back with an arrow and was still walking around with it sticking out of my chest. My breath came in gasps.

"Where are the signs?" I asked over and over again in panic. "Where are my signs?"

It became a drumbeat in my mind. For three years I had witnessed the five-fold ministry function, but I felt as if I were still in spiritual kindergarten. If I had been called to be a prophet, where was my prophetic gift?

"God!" I cried. "Let my enemies be scattered. Shut the mouths of my critics. Reveal signs and wonders in my ministry! Vindicate me! Defend me! Rescue me! I can't do this alone!"

Chapter 5

Called to the Growing Edge

*Also I heard the voice of the Lord saying: "Whom shall I
send, and who will go for Us?"
Then I said, "Here am I! Send me."
—Isaiah 6:8*

That agonizing cry for *charisma*—the evidence of God's
grace flowing through me—did not go unheeded. The
power did come. Signs did follow.

A voice from heaven comforted and scolded me. The
Lord said, **"Rachel, Rachel, quit your weeping!"**

I understood the Lord immediately even though the
wording was King James English. God speaks in your
own heart-language, whatever it is! By this point, my
heart was so immersed in the *King James Version* of the
Bible that it was normal for God to speak to me in quaint
old English phrases. I was even dreaming in Elizabethan
prose!

However, God also spoke to my heart in other ways:
through prophecies of friends, in the street language of
my old Detroit neighborhood, through advertising art
and signs, song lyrics, and even popular Christian books.

The more sensitive I became to the Lord, the more I
learned to hear his voice in "irregular" ways. This was
also a little scary to me. I wanted to be sure that God was

truly speaking. I wanted to avoid mistaking my imaginations for revelations. I learned to apply a three-way test:

First, **is the word consistent with the written Word?** You can be sure that real communications from God will always be right in line with what the Lord has already revealed in Scripture.

Second, **is the word confirmed by *"two or three witnesses"*?** (See Matthew 18:16; 2 Corinthians 13:1.) Whenever the Lord gave me a word, I found it always repeated through separate channels. Various people who don't know me or one another, would gave the identical word of confirmation. Sometimes confirmation came in different languages, countries, even years apart!

Third, **had I discerned the Spirit?** Gradually, I got better at differentiating between my own spirit and the Spirit of the Lord, between demons and the voice of the Lord. I never trusted my feelings alone—no woman should. I always checked with others. Discernment itself is a spiritual gift. I learned to submit my revelations to those whom I knew had it.

But there was no mistaking the voice of God this time. The Lord wanted me to quit mourning my imagined lack of power and start moving out in obedience. He promised the gifts would follow—and follow they did!

A Gift of Spiritual Power

My prayer was answered dramatically early one Tuesday. The phone rang. My Jewish girlfriend, Paula, asked me to join her at Zion Evangelistic Temple in Clawson. The Bible study was held in a cedar-paneled chapel that sat about 200.

Brother Gardner, who pastored the flock, deliberately avoided a fixed program on Tuesdays. He never scheduled a speaker and always began by waiting on the Lord with an extended time of praise and worship. Like the maidservant watching the hand of her mistress in Psalms, he watched the hand of God. Pastor Gardner let the Lord set the agenda and direction. He was a sensitive leader, inviting all to share according to 1 Corinthians 14:26, *"Whenever you come together, each of you has a psalm, has a teaching, has a tongue, has a revelation, has an interpretation. Let all things be done for edification."*

This day, the sacrifice of praise came differently and easily. The clichés were gone. The Holy Spirit come over me in wave after wave of power. A beautiful, lilting melody began to go up from the group. One voice would take over when another paused, replying and harmonizing with each other in endless worship. It was a new, free-form improvisation of song and adoration that we started to call "singing in the Spirit." At times, it seemed like the angels joined our chorus—or we joined theirs! Both were probably true.

In the midst of this intense devotion, I began to feel the compassion of Christ attracting me to a certain woman who appeared to be healthy. "Oh, she's so sick," I said through a word of knowledge and revelation from the Spirit.

Hot Hands

Then a supernatural love filled me. My hands began to tingle as if they were on fire. I felt the healing virtue of Christ literally pulsating in my fingers. As I laid my hands on her, I felt power flow out from me into her. The woman instantly fell down, overcome by the power of the Spirit.

This had never happened in my ministry before. Made bold by this sign, I began to walk around the room, laying hands on others. Soon almost everyone was on the floor, unable to stand in the holy presence of God.

I was overwhelmed at this demonstration of power. Probably, the disciples felt the same way when they came back exclaiming to Christ that *"even the demons are subject to us in Your name"* (Luke 10:17). I felt certain that God had used this specifically to answer my prayers for signs to follow.

Turning my eyes upward to worship the Lord, the praise was so pure and strong that my spiritual eyes were opened. I was actually able to see sound waves carrying our prayers into heaven.

That day, something was birthed into my ministry that has never been broken. It was the proof I needed. God assured me that He had endorsed my ministry with power from above.

Following the Revival Move of God

But God was relentlessly moving me on to my next assignment to bring in end-times revival. Spiritually discontent, restless and waiting on God, I still lacked specific direction. So I continued to meet with others at Bethesda, Zion Temple and in various house fellowships.

On Good Friday, brother Gardner called a special noon prayer service. Someone read a morbid account of Christ hanging on the cross, and a heaviness come into the room that was not from the Lord. I stood up in the Spirit and prophesied, **"Why look for Him among the dead when He is among the living? Jesus Christ is not dead. He is risen from the dead."** Immediately the sober spirit was lifted from the room. Everyone began praising the Lord with the kind of resurrection joy one would expect on Easter morning!

My gift brought awakening, new life, revival and renewal. The Lord showed me that I was to be a resurrection woman, not a Good Friday mourner! The Word of God in me is a living, explosive power that has to come out with rejoicing and life-giving power.

Afterwards my good friend and co-worker Reuben Aguas came to me. "Nancy," he said in a word of knowledge. "Your work is done here. We've heard you. Take the revival message on to others."

A Funeral at St. John's

Soon after, I received another life-changing call, this time from a troubled friend. Sylvia was a childhood playmate who was my best friend through our teen and college years. She had been a bridesmaid in my wedding.

We stayed in touch, even though we both had our own families and had grown apart. However, our friendship was strained on one point: any discussion of my rapidly growing faith was taboo. Sylvia was deeply involved in her own Episcopal church.

Now, her father was on his deathbed and had been in a coma for days. Sylvia asked if I would come to sit with her as the family waited for the end. Sensing a changed tone in her voice, I realized she was reaching out to me in a new way. Perhaps, I thought, that door to the spiritual dimension in our relationship was about to open. I rushed over.

It was an old-fashioned family death. The two sisters had set up a big bed in the living room that I remembered from our childhood days.

From the moment I walked in, the passing years seemed like only hours. There was a sense of eternity in the place. The coffee and doughnuts on the table were an unspoken invitation to sit down and pick up unfinished conversations from bygone years. And that's just what I did for a few minutes. I wondered if heaven would be like this.

Then something unexpected happened. God spoke. This time, it was the Lord talking to me sarcastically in my schoolgirl dialect of the 1950s! I recognized the tone as the same I used when my daughter left the dishes undone. God has an amazing sense of humor. *"When you're finished with your coffee,"* the Lord taunted me with a Detroit accent, *"would you mind..."*

I was gently rebuked. My forgotten assignment leaped to the front burner. Sylvia's dying father needed ministry now!

Ushering at Heaven's Gates

As the voice of God trailed off, my eyes instinctively darted to the still form on the big bed. It was time to forget the small talk and just do my Master's bidding.

Ignoring Sylvia, I fell on my knees beside his bed and spoke with a fiery anointing, "Dad, do you know that Jesus loves you?"

A tear rolled down his cheek. I realized that he could understand my attempts at witnessing even though he appeared to be completely comatose! The Word of God was getting through to him. He was alert and ready to receive the Word in his spirit. I ministered the comforting words of salvation as his daughters stood back and listened intently. The spirit of God was using me to send this man into eternity!

My prayers were being answered. God was moving in my everyday world. He brought me here to minister in the last moments of a man's earthly journey. Although I was not a pastor, God gifted me with a special grace to meet this man's deepest need in his dying moments.

God can use you anytime, anywhere—if you are willing to be a channel for His Holy Spirit! He will supply gifts you usually don't have to meet emergency needs.

A few minutes later, I heard Sylvia's relieved voice behind me. "It's okay, Dad," she said. "Go and be with your Maker." That seemed to be all the old man needed to hear. His last breath escaped. In the spirit, God allowed me to witness his soul leaving the body. I saw it as a little puff of smoke escaping his lips. It was as if he had finished his course in this world and was being born into eternity.

The blessed hope of our salvation became clear to me at that moment. I no longer feared death, only dying without that sense of accomplishment and peace which I had just witnessed.

While Sylvia called the ambulance, I stayed on my knees at the bedside to worship the Lord and thank Him for expanding my ministry into this intimate moment between death and life. Somehow, at that instant, I knew that this was exactly where Christ wanted me to be. It was as if Christ Himself were present in this visitation ministry.

Christ's words were so real: *"I was sick and you visited me...inasmuch as you did it to one of the least of these My brethren, you did it to Me"* (Matthew 25:36, 40).

Here Am I, Send Me!

The story continued later at the funeral. Strangely, God led the Episcopalian priest to choose Isaiah 6:8 for his homily. It hardly seemed like the text for a funeral.

However, he made the point that God wanted me to hear. *"Whom shall I send, And who will go for Us?"*

The question hung in the air as the pallbearers hoisted the body toward the waiting hearse. The presence of death made eternity seem so close and real.

Afterwards, I fell on my knees at the altar rail and sobbed. Bystanders must have mistaken me for a relative, but these were actually my cries of resignation and obedience. "Here am I. Send me!" I prayed, answering the Lord's question.

God was calling me again to go forward in service. I decided right then not to go back to being a pew-sitter in Bethesda or to any other established church. I would obey my original calling and go out to follow the move of God now, before it was too late. The Lord wanted me in the ministry. I simply had to be about the Father's business.

I no longer needed to wait around for more signs, special provisions or a complete blueprint. I had to launch out in faith. Nor did I have to wait for the further approval of men, ordination or a living allowance. God had blessed me with an adequate income and a supportive husband. I was free to obey if only I would!

Yet God doesn't particularly guide a bowl of fruit. It may make a beautiful still-life painting, but God hasn't called us to be simply on display for Him!

Obedience. Movement. Stepping out. God first requires us to make a free-will decision to act. Only when we've taken the risk of making mistakes in faith will He come alongside and give us mid-course corrections.

Like Riding a Bicycle

That funeral not only woke me up to the urgency of eternity, it got me moving out again. It pressed me into my second period of fervent, intentional witnessing. My search was over. The foundation was laid. Now I was determined to put into practice what I had learned, on my own, for the first time. I determined to use the gifts He had given to their fullest and then wait for more to come.

At first, no task was too small, no errand irrelevant. I responded to every call and invitation, learning to discern the voice of the Lord as I went along! When I moved in my own flesh or fell into one of the snares of the enemy, God spoke from behind me, *"This is the way, walk in it"* (Isaiah 30:21).

I moved out on faith, following what I called the bicycle principle. "How, Lord, can I learn to follow your Spirit?" I prayed.

The Lord answered me, **"It's like riding a bicycle for the first time. It looks like it will never stand upright. You just have to get on and get moving by faith. Once you have some momentum, the bike is ready to be guided, and I will direct you."**

I tried it, and it worked. As I obeyed His *"still small voice"* (1 Kings 19:12), the Lord would lead me one step further. Once there, I found the Lord was waiting with another command. Only then did I take the next step.

When Scripture says, *"Your word is...a light to my path"* (Psalm 119:105), it is not referring to a modern halogen lamp or battery lantern. The light in those days was just a flickering candle or oil-wick lamp. It gave the user just enough vision to see the path one step at a time.

The trouble with us is that we want to see everything all at once. We are like children who overload their plates with food; we don't have the judgment to know the difference between our appetites and the size of our stomachs!

Networking for Christ

I became an agent of revival and salvation as the move of God spread from town to town, person to person, house to house. Eventually, God used us to bring that move into every corner of Michigan.

My days were spent searching for "human connections," people who would be spiritual bridges to the next move of God. I never knew whom I would meet or where that would lead me, but I always knew I would meet someone! I had to be ready for instant obedience.

I determined to talk to anyone who would listen. I would take them as deep into the Lord as quickly as they were willing to go.

Once a wife or mother would invite me into her home, I started to work with everyone in the family, leading her children to Christ, then perhaps her husband, neighbors and friends. I witnessed as I went, imitating the way the apostles worked in the book of Acts. Often I would baptize a new believer in water and the Spirit only hours or days after they were born again!

In the early days of fresh faith, new converts are willing to obey the Lord in many areas of their lives quickly. Unlike older Christians, it doesn't take months and years of patient pastoring and counseling for them to go deeper in the Lord.

I started to make intense, short-term commitments to disciple people. I had seen my salesman husband work with that kind of fervent determination when a buyer was in the decision-making mood. Like Charles, I made many call-backs and did all kinds of follow-up by phone and mail, especially when I could see there was a lively interest in the Lord.

Routinely I would make two to three calls a week on new people. Often, at every meeting they would bring another new friend along! In this way, one decision for Christ might lead to three, six or twenty in month!

Hard on the Husbands

Often my intense interest in the lives of my new converts was misunderstood by jealous husbands and friends. The long hours we spent together, the hand-holding in prayer circles, the hugs and tears could easily be misunderstood. Sometimes it did seem that our love for one another was stronger and more demonstrative than that between a husband and wife. (Most husbands don't understand how emotionally starved their wives are, not for sex, but for the companionship and friendship they can find only in Christian fellowship.)

The devil often used these kinds of fears to derail and slander what God was doing in the revival during that decade. I remember one husband who confessed later that, when I first started having meetings in his house, he was afraid we were lesbians, "because of the way we were hanging on to one another!"

Thank God he didn't entertain those lies of Satan. His wife's *"chaste conduct"* caused him to be won *"without a word,"* as predicted in 1 Peter 3:1-2. Eventually, he was swept up into the revival along with his wife and went on to become an active Christian.

Women like Diane Ferkel opened whole communities to me in this way. I met Diane at a Women's Aglow luncheon. During the meeting, as we prayed and worshipped, Diane saw a vision of me with a wide gold band around my waist. The word "prophet" was written in bold letters on the band. God used this vision to ignite a flame in Diane that eventually spread to many of her neighbors in the little town of Leonard.

At least ten years younger than I, Diane was a typical postwar baby-boomer with little kids, a big van, and a huge house in the country. She lived in a really beautiful home at the end of a long dirt road.

She was a perfect counterpart for me, a practical leader who loved to live dangerously and take risks for God. She ventured onto any spiritual frontier that opened up and was always looking toward the next horizon. Diane's energy and itch to travel led us all over the map, not only to other homes, but to churches, house groups, and radio and TV stations. She was crazy for Christ. Together we turned her world upside down for the Lord.

Separating Religion from the Gospel

Just down the road from Diane lived her girlfriend Doris, a Roman Catholic in bondage to cigarettes. After Doris was born again, she invited other Catholic friends over to study the Bible, chain-smoking the whole time!

I laughed inside, thinking of how this kind of frontline evangelism would be unthinkable to many traditional Christians. Doris' cigarette smoking would have turned them away from her before she ever received a witness, and a soul might have been lost! How many millions do we lose in this way? I had to learn to overlook unpleasant habits, as well as cultural differences and weird lifestyles, in order to preach Christ.

Of course, Doris was eventually baptized and freed completely from her addiction to tobacco, but not before her entire circle of friends heard the Gospel. Many made decisions to enter into a personal relationship with the living Lord Jesus, too!

Meanwhile, I learned the art of stepping out of the way and letting God deal with addictions, fleshly sins and lifestyles that are displeasing to Him. The Holy Spirit convicts of sin and sanctifies. That's His job, not ours. Our judgmental body language, off-hand remarks, legalistic teachings and religious rituals can be deadly to new believers, driving as many people away from God as we attract.

Following the Harvest

Soon, we had visited every house on Diane's road. I'll never forget the twinkle in her eyes as she took me in ever-widening circles away from her home. "You haven't been this far before, have you?" she teased.

Sometimes, we would just pack the kids into the car and start driving, not even sure where we would begin that day. "Let's go to town," she would suggest innocently, "and pray for my neighbors." Those visits not only opened doors to her neighbors, but started a web of contacts and meetings that lasted for months. Diane, and a score of others like her, were among those who heard the trumpet's call and helped me launch nearly six years of marketplace ministries in the Detroit area.

She stayed with me until God called me to go to Springfield, a city that was finally too far away for even adventurous Diane! I had no friends there, no contact person. Yet God was calling. Did I dare go on alone?

Part Two:

"In All Judea and Samaria"

*But you shall receive power when the Holy Spirit has
come upon you; and you shall be witnesses to Me in
Jerusalem, and **in all Judea and Samaria,**
and to the end of the earth.*
—Acts 1:8

After a decade of discovery and training, Nancy Milsk
finally shifted into a second decade of ministry from the
late 1970s to 1989. This time it was mostly thankless,
behind-the-scenes service. She followed the revival move
of God throughout the state of Michigan and further
afield into her own Judean and Samarian regions.

She learned that the price of discipleship and renewal is often paid by suffering with Christ. Gradually
she found out how to intercede and meet God in the Holy
of Holies, discovering listening prayer and prophecy as
tools of service.

Chapter 6

Marketplace Ministries and Bathtub Baptisms

*And breaking bread from house to house, they ate their
food with gladness and simplicity of heart, praising God
and having favor with all the people. And the Lord added
to the church daily those who were being saved.*
—Acts 2:46-47

During the Springfield years, I learned that there are no
limits with God. Although we humans never cease trying, He simply cannot be boxed, packaged or restrained
by human cultures. Practices rooted in doctrine, gender,
race or religious tradition will not stop His move anymore than the grave stopped His resurrection.

I was a complete stranger in Springfield, arriving
alone without my usual co-worker. I came following the
move of God. When I left, there was a living, reproducing
church which touched hundreds of lives. It was truly an
anointed visitation—a church-planting mission.

Springfield was a bridge to new levels of love in
many of my dearest relationships—with Charles and the
children, as well as friends in Christ. It was also a time of
testing in which I experienced new levels of betrayal. I

had to learn again that my calling is to assist in the birth but not to cling to people and projects.

My marketplace ministries began while doing telephone counseling at channel 62, Detroit's all-Christian TV station. Edgar Bailey hosted the local Christian talk and variety show. One day he announced on the air that he had been invited to go to Springfield for a special outreach meeting. A faithful watcher named Sharon Bradley had rented a VFW hall for one night to bring Edgar's viewers together and to start a local fellowship to win her community to Christ.

"Join him," said the Spirit.

It sounded like such a bold, exciting idea that I immediately called Diane Ferkel. "Do you want to go with me to Springfield?" I asked. "Your house is on the way. Edgar Bailey is having a TV outreach there tonight!"

Diane hesitated a little, but finally said "yes." So we agreed I would drive and pick her up on the way.

Located about 90 minutes from Detroit, Springfield was a long drive for me. Without much of a living Christian testimony in the area, the spiritual needs were enormous.

Diane Is Grounded

When I arrived at Diane's, something was wrong. She wasn't dressed and ready to go.

"I can't go any further with you," said Diane. There was a finality in her voice. It wasn't like her to say anything like that. Diane was usually stronger than I was, more daring and outgoing, a real risk-taker. The Diane I knew went anywhere at anytime!

We stood there, both speechless. Her hair wasn't even ready. How could I wait for her? Didn't she know I couldn't go alone to a strange town?

I started to protest. I wanted to grab her by the shoulders and shake her into submission, but the Lord stopped me. *"Diane can't go any further with you,"* He said.

There was nothing more to say. I was going to be late if I waited another minute. My flesh cried out to stay with Diane and talk out her problem—to argue, to see what was wrong, to persuade her to change her mind. But I had to go. It almost seemed like the Holy Spirit was blasting my car horn, signaling me to get going. It was a clear choice between going with the Lord or staying with Diane. So I just blew Diane a wordless kiss and headed back to the car.

I was on my own, at least for tonight anyway. I was very uncomfortable. I am no "loner" by nature. Going solo was not just painful, but fearful. Yet I sensed this was a test of obedience.

My spiritual instincts told me that if I didn't go to Springfield right that minute, I was going to miss something. So I pushed the key into the ignition, consciously setting aside my fears in order to obey the Lord.

The Church Breaks Traditional Boundaries

The smell of stale beer and sweaty old men hung in the air of the Springfield VFW Hall. Across one side of the room was a long bar, closed for the night. (I guess the barkeeper had already figured out it was a waste of time to open tonight for this bunch of "Jesus freaks.") This was not exactly my idea of an ideal space for a gospel meeting, but later I found it was the only place available.

Recognizing Edgar's familiar face, I strolled across the wooden dance floor to join the small group of believers already formed into a pre-meeting prayer circle. Folding chairs had been neatly set up around the edges of the oak flooring, making a kind of theater in the round.

I sensed that somebody had worked, planned and prayed hard for this night, somebody who really loved her Lord and her community. Sharon Bradley turned out to be all that I imagined, a woman aflame for Christ. She was completely sold out to His service no matter what the cost. The rally went well.

During the altar service, there was great freedom to move with anointed authority. Everyone felt the power of God as we prayed, counseled and laid on hands with those who came forward to seek the Lord.

Afterward, Sharon came up and introduced herself to me with four words, "Nancy, I need help!" A bell went off in my spirit. I had met my first Lydia and received a "Macedonian call" to Springfield! (See Acts 16:9.)

It was the beginning of a powerful team. Sharon became my next best friend and sidekick in Christian service. Starting from her kitchen table, we saw the Holy Spirit spill out of old wineskins and flood into the marketplace of everyday life. We established home-cell groups in basements and living rooms all over town. We eventually organized a mission church together called the Springfield Christian Center which met in her basement.

Our ministry was in no way limited to Springfield. The little town became an operations base from which we reached out to Israel, New York and North Carolina. With Sharon and other women whom God attracted into our lives, I began to see God expanding the ministry.

Bathtub Baptisms and Homemade Church

It was above all a time to push back boundaries and establish new spiritual life. As the Lord poured out His

Spirit, we found any kitchen table could become an altar, any cellar a sanctuary, and any bathtub a baptistry. It was exciting to see the living church of Christ extend into parlors and kitchens, making everyday spaces sacred by the presence of the Lord.

We had homemade church. The Lord showed me how to use what was readily at hand to establish people and ministries. I learned to take a spiritual inventory of those we met. We tried to supply whatever was needed —on the spot, if possible.

God births life in true moves of His Spirit. Almost by definition, God's handiwork occurs outside the traditions of men, although it can come in older churches, too. I think the Lord delights in surprising us with His ways and skipping over ours!

Seldom have earthly traditions been more meaningless than during the 1970s revivals. Most of the time, we ministered from one living room to the next. That was probably the only way it would have worked. The sheep were scattered, wounded and alienated from the churches. These were mostly hurting women who needed ministry in the intimacy of a friend's house.

The mood was usually joyous. Around kitchen-table altars and coffee tables, women are not intimidated into silence. When we celebrated communion, it was really a celebration! Spontaneous songs and hand-clapping, informal prayer and worship were routine.

We planned liturgies for the unchurched. Baptism, communion, dedications, house-blessings, and footwashings were all part of our happy folk rituals.

I operated like a spiritual midwife during most of our visits. I wasn't there to control the situation, but to facilitate. I would talk, pray, teach. As we interacted, I would discern needs and unspoken heart-cries in the women.

As the Lord revealed the secrets of a seeker to me, I would bring a simple teaching from the Scripture. Then, I usually challenged the person to deal with it right then and there in obedience and faith.

If someone needed salvation, we went through the steps to being born again; if water baptism, we started the tub. If sin needed confessing, we knelt and prayed for forgiveness. If the person had never received the baptism in the Holy Spirit, we laid on hands. We prayed for physical healings and deliverance from habits, demons, sins and iniquity. We learned how to intercede and pray for compulsive needs, whatever they were! In medical terminology, I was a "spiritual paramedic" or "general practitioner."

Homes and hearts opened right up to us when we came to minister as woman to woman instead of clergy to laity. We tried to approach the ministry of Christ with the simple humility of "one beggar telling another where to find bread." As long as we kept this attitude, we had a growing community outreach.

Out of Town Overnight

Until Springfield, I didn't travel for Christ to distant towns or hold women's retreats. All my ministry was basically in my own neighborhood or in greater Detroit.

I'll never forget the first time I stayed overnight in Springfield. Charles and I had never been apart since we married except for his sales trips. I was always available for Charles and the kids when they reached out for me.

But this night, I could see I wasn't going to be able to make it home. (The idea that I'd have a pajama party for the Lord was exciting!)

"Charles," I said, when I got him on the phone, "it's so late, and I have a meeting in the morning. Don't you think it would be best if I stayed overnight at Sharon's house?"

The silence was ominous. Chuck didn't know how to handle this.

Then my daughter Lynn, who had been secretly listening on an extension phone, interrupted with an inspired comment! "Listen, Dad," she lectured, "when you're on sales trips, Mom has to stay home alone. Now she has to do her work for the Lord. It's the same thing."

That was breakthrough logic. It satisfied Charles, and the whole family soon accepted "sleepovers" as part of my ministry lifestyle.

Later as revival moved further out, I had to go on the road for several days at a time. We made trips all over Michigan and out-of-state as well. Springfield became the home base for all this travel.

When I found it hard to sleep in strange beds, I would often lay awake in prayer. Many times the Lord gave me a special word or insight for the next day in these night watches.

I actually began to look forward to these short separations for their devotional value. They provide many opportunities to grow closer to God through meditation, prayer and fasting. Romantic separations, like other kinds of fasting, are powerful aids in developing a closer walk with Christ, providing you follow Paul's advice to keep them short in duration and only by mutual consent.

To the Jew First

But it was more than just my trips. I feared some ice was forming between Charles and myself over my growing ministry. We both carefully avoided the subject, however. God used my mission to Israel to bring the problem into the open so we could deal with it.

From the earliest days of my conversion, God was constantly drawing me to witness to my many Jewish neighbors in Pinewood Manor. My daughter Lynn shared this attraction and love for Jews with me. Through one-on-one sharing, bumper stickers, tracts and even mailings, we made clumsy attempts to give the Gospel to our Jewish neighbors. Looking back, I realize that friendship evangelism would have been more effective than confrontation, but we were doing the best we knew how at the time.

When Edgar Bailey announced that he was planning a mission trip to Israel, I knew instantly I was to be part of the team. I took the Scripture, *"to the Jew first"* (Romans 1:16), very seriously. I wanted to intercede and witness in the Holy Land.

Sharon sat shaking her head in amazement that I didn't even have to think about the trip or talk it over with Charles. "Come on," I challenged her, "let's go together!"

By faith, I boldly pulled my check book out with a wide, sweeping gesture. But then, as I started to make good on my faith, my hands began to tremble and sweat.

I really did worry about what Charles might say. I've always been a submissive, sensitive wife. Fear overwhelmed me momentarily, but I decided to obey the Lord anyway. Calling on the Lord under my breath, I took a deep breath and wrote out a $100 check. Until then, that was the biggest step of seed faith I had ever taken.

As I suspected, it wasn't easy on Charles. He really didn't understand me this time. "What are you running to Israel for without me?" he asked plaintively, with all his emphasis on the two words "without me." Charles and I had enjoyed some of the best times of our lives traveling overseas together, and we had often talked of a trip to Israel.

I understood how he felt. But I was not planning a Holy Land holiday. This was a mission to share Messiah with the Jews.

While Charles didn't forbid me to go, he refused to give me a penny. His attitude was that if God had truly called me, then God could pay for the trip. My heart sank. Without Charles' help, there was no human way I could ever come up with the funds I needed.

I did the best I could, secretly saving some grocery money and selling some jewelry my father had made for me as a child. But I was still $900 short.

My faith was fading fast, and the air between Charles and me was getting frostier by the day. Yet I knew that I really was obeying the Lord in this matter. Like Shadrach, Meshach and Abed-Nego before the fiery furnace, I knew that somehow God would deliver me.

The Test of Our Love

Up until this time, Charles was mostly a curious onlooker at the amazing events that were going on in my life. He watched as a swirl of religious activity swept around his feet, much of it right in our home. People were getting saved in our living room. The sick were healed. Folks were being filled with the Holy Spirit. My kitchen often looked more like an office than a place to prepare food!

Charles watched it all silently—missing nothing, but barely commenting. At first, he would not commit himself to supporting me openly, yet he did nothing to stop me.

I prayed that he would not see this as just one more fad in my life. I was not going mad with religion. I was determined, steadfast. Christ had simply become the most important person in my life now, even though I loved Charles and the kids more than ever before. I hoped that they could all see this.

However, I was still fearful. I had not yet told him about my private water baptism or call to the ministry. I didn't feel free to be transparent about all this with him, but I was sick of keeping secrets. I had already seen the lack of honesty about the move of God break up other marriages and relationships. I had to come out of the closet and tell him the truth.

Finally, one night I broke down in tears. I couldn't hide my ministry and walk on eggshells around him anymore. I didn't want to offend him or lose his love, but I had to be honest with him no matter what happened.

"Charles, I am called to the ministry," I pleaded my announcement. "I want you to go before me. I want to be submissive. Please don't prevent me."

Something snapped in Charles when I said that. "I wasn't coming against you, and I'm not opposing you," he shot back. "Do you think that's what I was doing?"

Suddenly I saw the truth. He really wasn't hindering me and hadn't been all along. I knew he meant it. I was imagining a resistance that wasn't there!

That declaration from Charles was like the Magna Carta of my ministry, a bill of rights for the work God was doing in me. A rush of relief flooded my soul. The Israeli crisis had brought us to a boiling point in our relationship. Now, I knew where I stood. I had my husband's endorsement and blessing. Truly, the heart of the king is in the hands of the Lord. I can't imagine how I would have handled a situation where Charles stood in the way of my calling.

But even though I had his blessing, I noticed that the money for the trip was still not forthcoming! Charles was waiting to see if this was really from God. He wasn't exactly putting out a fleece consciously, but he was folding his arms and standing back.

That was a good thing because God had other plans to teach us all a lesson! He was going to provide the $900 for me through His own means. This had never happened to me before.

Remember, Sharon didn't have the money either. This meant $400 to cover her ticket, plus $900 for me!

The miracle came with a knock at Sharon's door. There stood a strange man holding an envelope. "I want to apologize," he explained. "You see, I'm a logger, and my men cut down thirteen trees on the back of your property a while back without your permission. Here's all I can afford to pay."

Thrusting the envelope into her hands, he abruptly left. Inside was a check for $1,300. Sharon used $400 for her fare and gave the other $900 to me as a gift for the trip!

Charles was totally awed. It was an astonishing sign of God's provision for the Israel mission.

From that moment on in our relationship, there was no longer any question that the call of God was on my life. I no longer had to struggle for words to explain it, nor was there any question of competition between the needs of God's people and duty to my husband.

Tearing Down Strongholds

Israel wasn't the only place God sent us to tear down strongholds of Satan that stood against the true church of Christ. One of the most bizarre missions was to Heritage Village and the PTL Club in Charlotte, North Carolina. On this amazing trip the Lord revealed His plans to bring down the TV ministry then at the very zenith of power and popularity.

This supernatural revelation came years before the terrible sex and money scandals exploded—the ones that eventually destroyed the ministry and helped send Jim Bakker to prison. It was my first taste of the powerful impact that intercessory prayer and prophecy teams can have.

It all started when Elaine Bell from Port Huron called. She and some girlfriends were driving down to Charlotte in a huge recreational vehicle. They had room for me! "Would I come?" I jumped at the opportunity.

It was January and bitterly cold. Only one of us had the courage or training to drive such a mammoth RV. It seemed to be the biggest thing on the road, more like a house on wheels than a bus!

We stopped often to rest and pray. We had hour after hour of awesome prayer and revelation. Everyone took turns ministering in the Spirit, often acting out specific prophecies and revelations for each other.

We even had a footwashing service. There was a remarkable spirit of harmony and intimacy. By the time we arrived in Charlotte, we were totally bonded. I have never seen a team of intercessors melt into one spirit in Christ so quickly!

Prophetic Predictions

Heritage Village was practically closed down. None of the summer activities were functioning yet, and so the theme park was practically deserted. In fact, Jim and Tammy Bakker weren't even there.

While the campgrounds were deserted, we still could not find a place to pray at first, so we rode the trams and joyfully prayer-walked the 2,200 acres. We were like the early disciples at Pentecost, literally drunk in the Spirit.

I'm sure that anyone who saw us would have thought we were crazy.

Then the Lord began to give us each separately the word that all we saw would be altered and changed. The PTL Club would crumble and be torn down.

The Holy Spirit had us stand in front of buildings and tear them down in the Spirit. One of the strangest commands was to remove in the Spirit the names—the little bronze plaques with the names of contributors—from the buildings.

We obeyed without understanding. Years later, I found out that the New Heritage Carolina Corporation bought the property, pledging not to solicit or accept donations for its operations! Never in a million years would we have imagined that bankruptcy courts were going to take Heritage USA away from the donors who built it and turn it into a business!

Marketplace Ministries

It was also at Heritage USA that God made Mark 16:15-16 real to us for the first time. In the *Living Bible*, Christ said, *"You are to go into all the world and preach the Good News to everyone, everywhere. Those who believe and are baptized will be saved. But those who refuse to believe will be condemned."*

While travailing in prayer, I glanced outside the RV and saw a trailer nearby with the words "Free Spirit" printed on back! It was no coincidence.

"Nancy," God said, ***"make those words your motto in ministry. Remain free, preaching the Gospel and ministering in the marketplaces of this world."***

As if to confirm His word, only minutes after I delivered this message to our team, God led us to a seeking soul as we walked through the lobby of the PTL Club studios! "Okay, Nancy," laughed one of the women, "this is your first marketplace ministry!" And why not? Since then, God has led me to use foyers, waiting rooms, the supermarket and even the post-office line as opportunities to witness.

Christ did much of his earthly ministry through such casual encounters. He was not limited to a temple or synagogue. We must be always alert for such divine appointments. God can lead anyone into our pathway at anytime, anywhere.

This word from God was so powerful that for the rest of the week, we turned our RV into a mobile evangelistic center. Unbelievers found Christ daily, and we did all kinds of counseling and ministry in that vehicle.

The lesson was clear. Even when you don't have an altar or formal counseling room, you can still find a place to meet God. He'll not only go with you into the marketplace, but He'll also provide a closet somewhere to find Him. It may be at your kitchen table, in the cellar or the attic. It may be a 5:00 AM in the morning or at midnight. Be ever alert for such sacred times or spaces, and you will find them. Even our Lord slipped away to find secret places and hours to pray.

Liberty or License

You know you're really dealing with the Holy Spirit when He burdens you to pray for the nations—not just your home town and native area—but the whole country, foreign lands, continents and people groups.

God desires the nations. Christ came for all the 24,000 people groups of this world. God promised

Abraham, the father of faith, that his seed would bless all nations.

A Christian should read the newspaper, watch TV, and listen to the radio differently than an unbeliever does. If done prayerfully, God can communicate all kinds of instructions.

As the 1970s dragged on, the news reported a country sinking deeper into crime and economic recession. Judgments from God weighed heavily on the nation.

Revival in America, not just Michigan, became critical in our prayers. My natural man wanted to pray for the capital of Washington, but God kept impressing the city of New York on me. I didn't understand very much about spiritual warfare then, but I knew one thing: in war, you have to listen to the commander. So I began to obey the Lord and pray for New York City, even though I had never been there.

In my prayers I began to see visions of a great darkness over New York. I saw a huge idol there—in fact, many idols that God wanted to tear down—but one that was much larger than all the rest. The Lord said it had to be torn down before the present move could spread to all of the United States. I began to realize that somehow, New York was the imperial city for demonic forces in the USA. It was then the nerve center of sin and rebellion for the whole country. The political capital of the nation is Washington, but the spiritual capital is New York!

With one of my best girlfriends, I felt God was attracting me to go and cast down the idols of New York. Where would we start? What was the biggest idol in America?

The Lord showed us that the Statue of Liberty needed to be torn down in the Spirit. The idea shocked me. It seemed so unpatriotic at first. I had never considered the Lady with the Light to be an idol. But the

Lord told us in our spirits that as long as it stood proudly, defying God, revival power would be blocked.

So as crazy as it seemed, we jumped in my car and drove overnight to New York City from Detroit. I had never been to New York Harbor before, but we parked our car in Manhattan and followed directions to the ferry.

Walking the frightening streets of Times Square and the lower East Side in the mid-70s revealed the depths to which any city or people can fall if Satan is not check-mated in the spirit world. The open homosexuality, por-nography, prostitution and violence of New York made it seem like a trip to hell. Truly, we realized that the "Queen of New York" had attracted people who came there not for freedom to be righteous, but for a license to sin. New York openly pursued and portrayed every kind iniquity of mankind's fallen nature.

To buy it back and repossess it for the kingdom of God, we needed to cast down every high imagination that vaunted itself against the Lord. So we prayer-walked our way around the city. We held Jericho marches and prayer vigils not only at the Statue of Liberty, but at Ellis Island, the United Nations and the World Trade Center.

While it seemed strange that God would send us half-way across the country to New York, I have since found many other Christians who had similar leadings and revelations during the same period. When you are one with the Lord in prayer, you can be sure that you are praying with angels, the whole church and thousands of unknown individuals whom God is uniting with you.

God did move nationally after that. The same move of God that we experienced in Michigan exploded all over the United States. What was happening in Springfield and the Detroit area was being repeated all over the country! Even the media reported it.

The Born-again Movement

In the late seventies, even the news media began recognizing something amazing in the spiritual world. National magazines, newspapers and television discovered us.

The world sat up and took notice. God was doing something new. Suddenly their eyes were on the Lord's new move and His people. Much of the early media coverage was almost reverent, not the mocking exposé-style journalism that would later announce judgment and destruction on big-name tele-evangelists.

I think the reporters knew that they were dealing with reality, a genuine move of God among the grass roots of our society. Suddenly, being born again was cool.

Campus Crusade launched the "I Found It!" campaign that fed the flames of God's revival move. Even presidential candidate Jimmy Carter grabbed headlines as a born-again Christian, as did Ronald Reagan following him.

Those were heady, exciting days. Millions of people had to recognize that God was alive and moving in America. Out of this move came thousands of new congregations and renewal in many of the older ones.

Christianity was breaking out of the four walls of the churches. This movement was not orchestrated by professional clergy or even evangelists. It was essentially a movement of the Spirit spreading uncontrollably as one individual witnessed to another.

This happened because we saw ourselves and everyone we touched as missionaries. Our home Bible studies, evangelism meetings and worship services were not an end in themselves, but simply tools to help us reach out to neighbors.

In traditional churches, valid programs of nurture, teaching and worship are too often substituted as an end in themselves. The "something for everyone" programs can become like religious drug addiction. By sidetracking the Holy Spirit in this way, it is easy for program-oriented churches to prosper and grow in numbers, but only at the expense of losing the true Lordship of Christ.

We tried not to lose the militant, others-orientation that comes from focusing all programs around loving obedience to the Great Commission. When nurture, care and worship programs are divorced from evangelism, they fall away from the move of God.

The chief characteristic of the move in the 1970s was that each new convert was immediately turning around and bringing a friend next week! Real life multiplies and divides, it doesn't add and subtract.

Such zeal cannot be contrived or worked up. In the move of God, the Holy Spirit empowers and motivates this amazing hunger after God. When we see the hot lava flowing from the volcano of God's love, we need to yield to that force. We must simply merge our spirits with His, flowing with Him through obedience.

A Spiritual Split

The time came when I realized that my work in Springfield was over. I wanted to follow the move; Sharon wanted to build the church. For about six months, I uneasily tried to hold on because we had been through so much together.

But the truth was plain. My friend was established and really didn't need me anymore. She was looking for pastors and teachers instead. The intercessor-prophet's foundational building team was settling down and being transformed into a structured institution. When that happens, there is less and less need for the ministry of a prophet and a greater need for elders and deacons.

The Lord had sent me to set up the scaffolding, and that was done. My ministry wasn't clicking anymore. Other gifts in the five-fold ministry now took pre-eminence. It really was time to move on, but neither of us knew how to make my exit graceful.

For the first time, there was competition between us. The struggle for control was unbearable. While I understood this intellectually, it was much harder emotionally. The pain was almost like a spiritual divorce or losing a spouse, made worse because we resisted.

Prophets must know when to let go and move on to God's next place of service.

Chapter 7

Five Women in St. Clair

No one, having put his hand to the plow,
and looking back, is fit for the kingdom of God.
—Luke 9:62

The burden of Springfield stayed strong in my spirit. Fleeting remnants came back to haunt me even after I was well established elsewhere.

A friend had told me that we have to wait on the Lord for the release from a spiritual burden. The Springfield church was probably the deepest bond I had ever formed with a group. It hurt to be separated from them. I began praying daily for the Lord to relieve my burden and the ache in my heart.

Even though I knew it was time to go, the thought of being without friends, without a ministry, without a busy schedule, without folks who needed me was very frightening. This was a kind of spiritual empty-nest syndrome! Actually, it was worse. I was in deep grief. I was losing my babies. No one needed me anymore.

Closure came one morning as I sat alone at my kitchen table, wallowing in self-pity. I offered the sacrifice of praise, thanking the Lord that my work in Springfield was done. Still, I had no place to go.

The strong, clear notes of a bird's song broke the silence. Looking out my kitchen window, I saw a brilliant red cardinal perched on the very top of a tree. God spoke: *"That's you! You're My little bird. You have to keep singing the notes I give you. When you let go of Sharon and Springfield, I will meet your need."*

"Okay, Lord," I replied. But, I thought to myself, He better meet my need fast!

Then within seconds the miracle phone call came. It was Gail Britz, an old friend from St. Clair. Coming when it did, her words were an extension of God's voice. It was as if He started the conversation in my spirit and ended it on the phone!

"Nancy," she said, "a group of us are waiting on the Lord in St. Clair—just a kitchen-table prayer meeting. Would you come up and pray with us?"

So Gail was my next Lydia, and the move was to St. Clair! I knew it was God. I didn't need to hear another word. My spirit leapt, responding to the call.

At Gail's Kitchen Table

Gail Britz had a modest, almost Spartan house. The siding was made of tar-paper shingles, the kind that look like imitation brick. A frame structure on the wrong side of the tracks, it shook as 100-car coal trains rumbled through the sleeping town each night. The entrance was from a side door that opened into a mud room covered with old-fashioned linoleum flooring. Just up a short flight of stairs was Gail's kitchen.

An immense bathroom opened off the kitchen. It was perfect for us. There was a giant, old-fashioned bathtub that stood up off the floor on claw-like legs. We baptized all her kids there and half the neighborhood as well!

The room was so huge that we actually met in there following baptisms. I vividly remember the kids stepping over praying forms to use the facilities. We were so caught up in the Spirit that no one even paused when the toilet flushed!

In the kitchen, the wire-backed chairs looked like they came from an old ice-cream parlor. Long periods of tarrying before the Lord were the rule rather than the exception at Gail's kitchen table. Here we formed a Jesus Circle and first experienced prolonged spiritual warfare.

Gail was radiant in her spirit and had a heart after God that just wouldn't quit. I baptized her and felt like her spiritual mother in some ways, but she was growing beyond me in others. Life flourished around her open heart and home, and it became a house of prayer as she grew more intimate with Christ.

A Fiery Vision

I often arrived early in the day to pray and drink tea with Gail before the core group arrived for intense waiting and worship. These meetings often lasted past midnight with people coming and going.

One night, things didn't begin moving in the Spirit until about 10:30. I received an amazingly clear vision. It was like dreaming with my eyes open.

Suddenly I saw a group of believers meeting in a burning church building. I shrieked in horror. The people were burning to death. The vision was so real that I could feel the heat and smell the smoke. "Get out! Get out!" I shouted. "The church is on fire, and you're going to burn up!"

My hysteria terrified the group. But Gail stayed calm, always willing and ready to receive anything from the Lord. She was sitting right across from me at the table. She reached over, took my trembling hands in hers and soothed me, saying, "Now Nancy, just relate the vision as you see it happening."

I began to share as it unfolded before my spirit. "I'm screaming at them," I said. "I'm warning them that the church is on fire and they're going to burn up, but they won't move. I cry as the flames burn their flesh and they start to die one by one.

"The church is in a valley, and rain starts to come down from the mountain. When the fire quits, I start to pull the bodies out with my hands, laying them on the grass one by one. When all the dead are removed, I cry out in prayer, but I can't revive them.

"Then the rain starts again. Somehow the water brings the bodies alive! But they are walking wounded. Their burns are open sores.

"I become a sheep dog and start nipping at their heels, gathering them together and lining them up in ranks. When they are all lined up and in place, I realize who these people represent. These are the wounded sheep of the current move, the surviving sheep of the slaughter.

"In the form of a sheep dog, I drive them into a huge human body. Then they begin to file into the body through a door in the back. Somehow as they enter, all merge into one flesh. The wounds disappear and are absorbed or healed by the whole body. The body begins to grow bigger as each person is added.

"The body becomes glorious. Big. Strong. White. Radiant like the sun.

"Finally, all the survivors are inside, and I shut the door. They have become unified—one mind, one body, one voice. The whole body quivers. All the voices merge into one great voice that shouts 'Jesus Christ is Lord!'"

Hound of Heaven

Sometime after this vision of my ministry—which needed practically no explanation or interpretation to our group—Charles and I were at Greenfield Village in Dearborn, Michigan. There, outside Henry Ford's museum, we actually saw a real sheep dog corralling lambs.

He ignored the huge crowd of spectators and their applause. I never saw anyone, canine or human, so completely devoted to his work. He crouched, crawled, lunged, nipped. He maneuvered around the sheep and surprised them one at a time, driving them into the corral until he had every lamb in place.

Since God gave me this vision of my ministry, I found I'm not the first to see myself as a sheep dog! Dorothy Sun, a Chinese missionary from Shanghai also describes seeing herself this way. Other Christians with similar revelations have included Saint Dominic. That 12th-century preacher envisioned his Dominican missionary order as the "hounds of heaven," sent out by God to call people to Christ.

Acting Out Intercession

There were five women in the core group at Gail's house: Carol, Doris, Gail, Shirley and me. The five of us learned to pray as one—but not before I humbled myself.

One night, early in the move at St. Clair, the group started to pray through "grocery lists" of requests. I had always hated that kind of prayer. I had revival on my heart. While I often joined with intercession groups, I grew restless in any protracted prayer time—especially "bless me" clubs.

"I'm really not into this," I announced during a pause. "I'm more called to prophecy. I can't take anymore. I'm going home!"

"Bye!" waved Gail, returning to prayer without looking up. Miffed, I got up to leave and put on my coat.

Then God spoke, *"Nancy, Gail is going to teach you intercession."*

Outside in the car I broke down and cried, "Lord, I baptized her. I know more. I'm older. What can she teach me?"

"I have gifted her with intercession," said God. *"She will be your teacher. You're going to have to humble yourself and learn from someone younger than you."*

The next day I came back and confessed my need to Gail. "God told me I've got to learn intercession from you," I said. "Will you teach me how to pray?"

Gail was standing at the sink. "Oh!" she cried, gasping for breath and holding her stomach.

"What's wrong?" I asked.

"I feel like I'm having a contraction, like a baby is coming!" Gail fell to the floor and began weeping, doubling up in pain and holding her stomach.

Pain and tears are often part of intercession. We have to learn to lament, grieve, regret and repent if we are to go deep into the heart of Jesus. Many intercessors suffer cramps and afflictions in prayer.

In Psalm 56:8, David tells how God keeps our tears in His bottle, records them in a book, and numbers our wanderings! Groans and cries may seem like foolish hysterics to outsiders, but God counts every one!

So in this very emotional and physical way, Gail led me into prayer. This was my training period in intercession. I would join her, crying real tears and weeping for situations that the Spirit of God showed us were on His heart at the time. Not a tear drop was lost.

Corporate travail with the group came next. Travailing prayer is not just for women. Throughout the Bible and history, real men of God have travailed in prayer. Gail's husband frequently joined us, as God broke our hearts with His love.

Often, our sessions were so intense that we lost all track of space and time. Full days or nights of prayer were frequent. One extraordinary time lasted three days.

During corporate travail, the bonding was so close it was not uncommon for one intercessor to begin a sentence and another finish it. One asked a question and another answered. One would give a word and another would add some knowledge to it.

For example, I might say, "Arizona."

Carol would answer, "Indian spirits," and go on to explain something. Prayer sessions like this frequently led to prophecies, instructions and commands.

We would pray-read newspapers and letters from Christian ministries. Maps and Bibles were vital. We would frequently center a whole session around a map. God often gave directions related to places and people.

Prayer Tools

Praying before an open Bible brought many revelations as the Holy Spirit Himself was present and would illuminate a text. Details unseen previously would grab our attention. It is much easier to understand a passage and apply it when you pray-read.

Instructions received in corporate travail became our marching orders. It was normal to see prophecies fulfilled as we went out on visitation trips to local churches, individuals and spiritual strongholds.

Obedience was important. We learned to sit when the Holy Spirit said sit, stand when He said stand, go when He said go. In this way, intercession trained us in spiritual sensitivity.

Gradually, Carol and I became the scouts for the Jesus Circle at Gail's—the eyes and the ears of the ministry. We received anointings and assignments from the group. Prayer was a springboard for ministry. God had blessed me with another best friend in ministry. Carol and I became almost inseparable for two years.

Spiritual Headquarters

So St. Clair became a spiritual operations base for us, our spiritual-warfare headquarters. First, we trained the big guns of intercessory prayer on people, places and problems. Only then would we go in for ground combat! We followed up our prayer attacks with visitation and ministry in spiritual gifts.

What we saw in the spirit, we applied in the natural. As we followed God's instructions, we would bring revival everywhere we went.

Sometimes we testified and shared in local gatherings when invited to speak. Many times we would just worship with the believers and fellowship afterwards. These visits led to contacts who networked us into prayer groups and house fellowships.

Sometimes, our assignment would be simply to stand outside a place of darkness, such as a palm-reading parlor, casting down the works of Satan. We learned that some places of darkness have waited hundreds and even thousands of years for intercessors to come and break the power of an ancient curse or spell. We broke all kinds of spiritual bondage and took authority over evil spirits wherever they manifested themselves.

Carol was a big, strong, Russian-American woman with the courage to lead and take me to places where the Spirit was leading us. Together we made an excellent team. She was Moses, and I was Aaron. Our relationship in ministry was symbiotic. We needed each other. It is always wise to remember your order in spiritual warfare and practice mutual submission.

We learned to possess the land wherever we went. Anointing our feet with the *"preparation of the gospel of peace"* (Ephesians 6:15), we claimed territory as we pray-walked our way through it.

The Lord regularly revealed emblems and idols that needed to be taken down in the spiritual realm before He would be free to come and work in a place or situation. Demons love to animate sculpture and monuments. It was Carol who went with me to New York to pray at the United Nations to release revival to all the peoples of the world and to take down the Statue of Liberty idol, releasing the United States for the move.

New Life for a Cathedral

Learning to tear down these strongholds was terrifying for me. I'll never forget the time we visited a Roman Catholic cathedral to bring in charismatic renewal. I had never ministered in such a public place before. For me this was real guerrilla warfare. I didn't have the courage to ask permission of the local priest.

Just inside the door was a bronze plaque memorializing the missionary bishop who had founded that diocese over 150 years earlier. It had a little map captioned with a description of the bishop's territory. The word "territory" blinked at me like a neon sign.

The Lord spoke, *"Nancy, I've been waiting 150 years for this man's stronghold to be broken. This is not his territory, but My territory. I want you to go into this church and worship me at the high altar."*

As I spoke out the Lord's command, Carol led the way toward the splendor of the high altar, all the time offering sacrifices of praise in a stage whisper! I halted, trembling. I looked up the steps. It was strange and forbidding. Wasn't that altar only for priests? What if someone came in and found us up there?

In a very inner-city Detroit voice, God spoke again, *"What's the matter? Are you afraid of lions or something? Go right up and stand at the altar. Break everything here that's not of Me and My Spirit."*

We obeyed. In prayer, we broke and cast down every image and tradition of man that wasn't of God. No one came in during the whole time we ministered.

Again the Lord spoke, *"Now, go to the pews. I want you to speak to each one of them. Command new life to come into My church."*

Carol walked down one side, and I walked the other. Laying hands on the pews as we went, we took authority over death when that assembly met. We ordered new life to come in as God commanded. Next, we cast out religious spirits. We were still alone. No one had yet entered the church. I breathed a little deeper.

"Now," said the Lord, *"Go to the holy water and shake it with your hands."*

We obeyed.

"Now, walk out," concluded the Lord.

Just then, my heart almost stopped beating as the monsignor entered the sanctuary, greeting us with a friendly, "Good morning, ladies!" I wondered if he could smell the fear and terror in my heart. As we raced down the steps after that, I felt like a naughty child, running from an abandoned house I'd entered on a dare.

We drove home to Carol's house and collapsed in exhaustion. "Lord," I prayed. "I hope all spiritual warfare is not going to be this exciting!"

Northern Starburst

The direction of our missions and witnessing assignments seemed to keep us moving northward. Then the Lord showed us this pattern was His.

As a ministry team, we were all in accord in the Spirit. Just as He promised in Romans 15:5-6, God gave us the grace to be *"like-minded toward one another... that you may with one mind and mouth glorify the God and Father of our Lord Jesus Christ."*

Gail related what she perceived in the spirit, "The Lord Jesus says, *'Look at the map one more time.'*"

She spread out the Michigan map. With a child's plastic ruler, she drew random lines. They all intersected at one point. We looked at the center of the starburst to see that the fulcrum point was Mount Pleasant.

So Carol and I began making prayer missions in the direction of Mount Pleasant, a lovely college town practically in the center of the state. But as yet we had no contacts there.

All Things Are Shaken

Then, mysteriously, Gail started to get sick. With her frequent hospitalizations, the group began to slowly break up.

We missed her. Gail was a peacemaker, settling problems between Carol and myself. The two of us had trouble submitting to each other. Gail was a good sound-ing board for us, a home base where we could always land for a cup of tea and some encouragement.

Then one day, I visited her in the hospital. A drastic deterioration in Gail's condition had taken place. Her ovarian cancer had spread beyond human treatment.

Gail was letting go of life. The fire was gone. I could see it. She prophesied to me that God was sending me to many nations and many places. She insisted I go alone. She no longer shared the vision. She was letting go of me. She knew I couldn't stay there and attend to her to the end of this life. My calling was not to carry and nur-ture her to death's door.

God confirmed the message: ***"She can't go any further with the move, Nancy. You have to go on alone."***

The others in our circle found that prophecy most painful to accept, especially in the terrible days that followed. One by one, personal tragedy struck each of us.

Tidal Wave of Tragedy

The others wanted me to stay put and fit in, to start to pastor the St. Clair group and hold them together, but I couldn't. I had to follow the move northward. All I could do was cry with them, pray for them and go on.

No one was more hurt than Doris. She was so disap-pointed in the group. When her house burned down, she looked to us for help, but we had nothing more to give. The St. Clair group simply didn't have the resources. We were not a church.

Shirley broke away next. We were sent on a prayer mission to Arizona, but she couldn't go with us. The next thing we heard, her little daughter had gotten her foot stuck it a motor bike. It had to be partially amputated. Shirley dropped out after that.

Then, I found out my daughter had secretly married and was expecting a baby.

We didn't know what personal attack would hit us next. It was a time of Job's trials. Our shields were down. Prayer times became crying times. I didn't accuse the Lord, but I couldn't understand why all these bad things were happening to good people.

God warned sternly, *"Nancy, keep your eyes on Me, and I'll take you through this time of sorrows. I'll watch over your family, finances and health. Just don't take your eyes off the move. Look to Me as your source and move ahead."*

Finally, we received the death blow to our little prayer circle. The news came that Gail had passed away. She had finished her work for the Lord on earth. For a time, her little house by the tracks had housed the school of the prophets, but now it was over.

At the funeral, the St. Clair Jesus Circle was all there for one final reunion. Afterward, we walked to the parking lot through a cyclone fence. The sound of the gate crashing behind me was loud and final, like the sound effect you always hear in prison movies when they slam the barred doors shut on a prisoner.

As the gate locked itself shut behind me, I heard the Lord say, *"Well, Nancy, that door is closed. Now it's time for you to go on and take this show on the road!"*

"Take the show on the road?" I laughed back. "Is that really you, Lord?" I asked, checking to make sure it was really God speaking my native dialect. The Lord sounded very Afro-American today! Very Detroit.

"Yes," repeated God, gently mocking me in His best Motown chant. *"I said it's time now to take this show on the road!"*

It was faith time again. I needed to go into the Holy of Holies and talk to the Lord about the needed finances if I were really going to be able to follow wherever God was leading me. I kept recalling His earlier words to me that He was appointing me to go to the nations. But I knew that it was God calling, and He would make a way somehow.

God had been providing for the ministry through Charles and the Milsk Company. But how would Charles react now when I told him that the Lord had been calling me to an extended outreach, perhaps overseas? I just had to close my eyes in faith and let God take over. I was going. He would provide.

Chapter 8

Taking Our Company for God

Believe on the Lord Jesus Christ, and you will be saved, you and your household.
—Acts 16:31

Charles stood by me. Through the changes and over the years, his constant faith rolled with the storms. As I struggled to grasp God's call for my life, he was always there with gentle, quiet support.

Without seminary or formal Bible school training, I lacked professional training for my ministry. Further, I had no real prophet to mentor me as Elisha had Elijah.

So everything God taught came the hard way through some dramatic successes, but mostly through disappointment, error, failure and rejection. All had to be learned as my family and our employees watched me publicly go through it in real-time everyday life!

They took their cues from Charles. His old-fashioned trust released me to the Lord for guidance along my spiritual journey. He set this faith pace when I'm sure neither he nor I fully understood what God was doing.

No matter how far I traveled for the Lord, I always knew that Charles was in the background supporting me.

There aren't many husbands who have the special grace to tolerate a wife on a mission, who will "cut her the slack" needed to keep irregular hours, travel and entertain so many strange and needy people.

God's Provision from the Family

I've never asked for the financial support of a church, denomination or big mission board. Instead, Charles and I have learned to claim the promises of God for both business and ministry needs.

Promises like Deuteronomy 8:18 have kept us going: *"You shall remember the Lord your God, for it is He who gives you power to get wealth, that He may establish His covenant which He swore to your fathers."* That Scripture has been the cornerstone of our financial policy. It is a marvelous, but conditional, promise.

Everything in this universe belongs to God. He has put it there to supply all our needs in order to give Him glory. When I started Trumpet Ministries, I didn't go out raising funds. Instead, I went into the Holy of Holies. All I needed was right there—the energy, favor, finances, power gifts, speaking gifts, wisdom and knowledge for the work. God showed me how he wanted to use Charles, the family and the Milsk Company in this ministry.

This Company Belongs to J. C.

The ministry has always had an almost symbiotic relationship with the company. Chuck's Dad, Robert, founded the Milsk Company in 1927. He spent his whole life building the foundations for what it is today. I don't think he consciously knew he was really building something for the Lord.

Although not born-again until the last hours of his life, Robert L. Milsk was a righteous, hard-working Jew. His immigrant parents brought him from Russia as an infant. Out of that experience, he was driven to build something really special in his new homeland.

While he rarely talked about his faith, Robert Milsk married Evelyn, a devout Dutch Reformed girl from Grand Rapids. Together they left a godly heritage in both family and business.

Chuck's mother once confessed to me that as a child she dreamed of being a missionary. Instead, she took vows to Robert and spent over fifty years working alongside him to establish one of the most respected electronics firms in the Midwest.

Charles, and my sons in turn, absorbed this sober dedication to the family business. The Milsk Company is like a family farm. Everyone still works at it day and night. But since Charles took over the company, we've seen two radical changes.

First, the company is no longer an end in itself. It is not simply a money-making machine. Charles and the boys openly boast that the company belongs to God. They are learning to operate it by spiritual principles. Every bit of knowledge we've acquired in the ministry about seed-faith, intercession and possessing the land is being poured into the company. We've been tearing down artificial barriers between the secular and the spiritual in our lives and the business.

Second, the company has become a dynamic base of provision for God's end-times move around the world. Because the family has stood with me in support of this ministry, I haven't had to spend time begging to raise money for our ministry. Thanks to my hard-working family, when God really says "go," I prayerfully pull out my checkbook and obey the Lord in faith!

I praise God that, thanks to the Milsk Company, I've never had to make a ministry decision motivated primarily by income. When I decided to write this book, for example, it wasn't because I needed to sell books for a living! It was an act of obedience to God.

The Blessings of Profit

Capital and profits are necessary blessings from God in our Christian lives and work. But Christ reserved some of His harshest judgments for religious leaders who become enslaved to them. Many Christian ministries have started out well but have fallen into this deadly trap, in part, because they haven't been blessed with a family business to support their basic needs as I have.

One of the women on our Mission to Moscow team believes God has created a personal land of Havilah for each of us. God has a place where it is said, *"the gold of that land is good!"* (Genesis 2:12). "I used to pray that God would sell some of the cattle He owns on a thousand hills," she laughed. "Now I just ask God to give me the wisdom and knowledge to know where the gold is!"

In the Holy of Holies, God answers prayers and shows each of us the location of our Havilah, and how to mine it for His glory. Much of my life is invested into the Milsk Company for that reason.

Ministry at Corporate Headquarters

Since I married Charles, I have always been involved in the day-to-day company workings. (When you marry a Milsk, you marry the family firm as well!) The more I ministered, the more I depended on the company to help.

My earliest memories of using the support services of the company date back to 1975, in the middle of our campaign to bring Billy Graham to Detroit. On my own time, I started making thousands of copies for our mailings.

The busier the campaign grew, the more I needed to borrow Milsk Company equipment. But I sensed that my extracurricular use of the office was being observed by Grandpa Milsk. I had crossed a certain line with my substantial use of equipment and supplies. I held my breath as I worked, praying for favor and claiming the continued use of the company for the Lord's work.

One day, during a particularly long copy run, Chuck's dapper father came over, scowling a little at me and the machine. I waited for the ax to fall, but he was struck dumb. Before walking away, he paused and whispered very quietly, "Okay, use the office."

I realized that I had just gotten his miraculous approval to use the office for the Lord's work. There was never a problem again. The office was the Lord's and available for His use at any time.

Possessing the Company for God

Later at Bethesda Temple, Mother Beall preached on the righteous man from Psalm 112:1-3, *"Blessed is the man who fears the Lord...His descendants will be mighty on the earth...Wealth and riches will be in his house."* I was transfixed by this amazing promise.

At the end of the service, Mother Beall called forward all the business owners who wanted the Lord to bless their businesses. In a moment I was on my feet, standing in the gap for Grandpa Milsk and Charles. "Our family and our family business belong to you, O Lord!" I confessed. It was a big turning point for me.

Later, I went into the boardroom and wrote out my declaration of faith on the company blackboard:

This company belongs to J. C.
Our borders will increase!

I was afraid to write "Jesus Christ" because at that time everyone in the industry still thought of our company as a strictly secular business.

I felt the Lord's presence with me. He spoke, *"What's the matter, Nancy? Are you ashamed of My name?"*

"No, Lord," I said, "I'm not ashamed of Your name. I mean, I don't want to be ashamed of Your name. I'm just afraid of what Chuck's dad will say—he's Jewish, You know."

The Word of God from Mark 8:38 came to me again: *"For whoever is ashamed of Me and My words in this adulterous and sinful generation, of him the Son of Man also will be ashamed when he comes in the glory of His Father with the holy angels."*

With trembling hands, I erased the "J. C." and wrote out His name in bold capitals:

This company belongs to Jesus Christ!
Our borders will increase!

My claim on the company did not go unchallenged. The words were quickly erased by staff members. But every time I passed that blackboard, I changed them back: **"This company belongs to Jesus Christ!"**

That was eighteen years before legal control of the company passed to Charles, but by faith I had already taken possession of the company for God.

In 1981, I came home from a convention with some "God Bless You!" stickers. They were pressure-sensitive labels. I began putting them on everything in sight. "God

Bless You!" began appearing on the sales bulletin board, on letters and all over. I wanted us to become a source of God's peace and prosperity, a company associated with God's favor and presence. But not everyone understood my "God Bless You!" campaign.

One day I overheard two of our employees talking about the blessing labels. One angrily asked, "Who's putting these crazy stickers up all over the place?"

"Oh, that's the boss's wife," came the reply.

I didn't hear another complaint after that! Rank has some privileges, and God will indeed bless us when we use our power and position to honor Him. It was another small step toward victory.

Over the years, I offered up hundreds, maybe thousands, of such little witnessing actions like that one, plus countless prayers for the company. But not every answer to prayer was an instant miracle. We always need to add patience to our faith when we launch out to possess our lands, businesses, families and organizations.

Lord of All

Only when Robert Milsk died at age 75 did the Milsk Company really started to become what it is today—a school of faith for the whole family and staff. Now, my sons acknowledge God as the source of their success, even to unbelieving clients and competitors!

The other day I walked through the office, past the old blackboard where my trembling hands once shook to write, **"This company belongs to Jesus Christ!"** Today, on that same blackboard is a list of prayer requests and praises. How many companies list prayer requests on the boardroom wall? How many stop the whole office to praise the Lord when a commission check comes in, a sales goal is met, or an award is received?

Among the posted items were grateful praises. Thank you Lord for: (1) $25 million in new sales; (2) wisdom regarding the Stewart account; (3) guidance in the Chrysler contract. Also listed were requests. Pray for: (1) new lines; (2) old accounts; (3) increased ROI; (4) buyers by name. Everyone we touch as a company is prayed for by name!

"The word of God and prayer are what keeps the Milsk Company ticking," says my son Ronnie. Even in dry periods and recessions, Charles and the kids are calling on the Lord and confessing His promises over the company's books, finances and sales. We pray-read the Book of Proverbs over all the Milsk Company affairs. That is the secret of our success.

Corporate Chaplain

"Not many companies have a corporate chaplain—or want one!" jokes Charles. But for many years now, I have officially been listed as the Rev. Nancy Milsk, Corporate Chaplain, The Milsk Company. I am available to Charles and the boys at any time for prayer.

Often, Ronnie or Steve will call me by car phone on the way to visit a client. "Mom," Ronnie will say, "in twenty minutes, I'm going to be meeting with Mr. Johnson at Ford headquarters. That will be 11:15. Can you be praying for me then?" We will usually agree together immediately, and I will again pray during the appointment. The boys pray before, during and after all meetings.

I also invest Scriptures into my sons, giving them a sticky note with a promise or proverb that applies to a goal or situation. They always know when I've been in the office. I go around the office sticking verses everywhere, putting faith goals on desks, calendars, bulletin boards and in certain files. These reminders alert us to pray again for what we've agreed for in faith.

Some targets are God's goals because we have believed together and made a faith covenant for them. I'll hear Ronnie or Steve say something like, "That $20 million is the Lord's" when planning the future. We believe in sanctified goals.

Sometimes I cut a verse out of the Bible, tape it on a card and send it over to one of the boys. Recently, I sent Proverbs 18:16 (TLB) over as God's solution to a certain problem. *"A gift does wonders; it will bring you before men of importance!"* As always, the Word of God works. In this case, a gift was sent which opened a long-closed door.

Charles knows that even when I'm not on the convention floor or at the company, I'm always in my Milsk Company office of prayer!

We're blessed to have a family business where we all know when there's a crisis or a blessing. We can get on our knees quickly. This is even more true when reaching sales goals. The victory is pretty easy to see. "It's all sales!" says Charles. "If you don't sell anything, the lights go out!"

As corporate chaplain, I pray regularly for all the lines we represent and each of our salesmen and employees. Of course, as I pray I remember my grandchildren, my daughters-in-law and daughter Lynn. Before my mother-in-law and Robert Milsk went to be with the Lord, they were part of my daily intercession as well.

The company has been a powerful source of unity and teaching in our family, as well as a source of supply to Trumpet Ministries and all our families. Instead of merely resisting the world, the Lord wants us to conquer and overcome it—and family businesses are a good way to do it.

Ron Applies His Faith

Ron was the first in our family to really grasp the significance of bringing the company in line with the Word. I remember when we first started to pray-attack problems. He realized everything we need is in Christ. Someone gave him a teaching tape on God's inexhaustible storehouse of everything we need: contacts, energy, faith, finances, health, knowledge, power and wisdom.

Together, Ronnie and I would determine what was needed and then pray it into existence. We started to shoot what we called "$100 Faith Arrows" at any stubborn problem. We would seek God's will and solution to the situation, as we planted a $100 seed gift in some ministry for the satisfactory conclusion. When we saw that a certain client or sales activity was no longer bearing fruit, we would prune it back as the Bible teaches or add fertilizer.

"Our competitors can't understand our success," Ron says. "They come against us with slander and that fails. They don't know they're opposing God's anointed."

Ron gets up each morning and puts on the full armor of God before work. "I use everything Mom taught me—obtaining the deed to the land, taking possession of it, finding the key that opens the door, favor, knowledge and wisdom. I do business using the principles of spiritual warfare.

"I also use the principles in my everyday life. Things are coming a lot easier. Instead of fretting and worrying, I put my problems in God's hands, and the job is done!"

Steve's Jesus Wall

Both Ronnie and Steve are operating in the power of the prophetic word. Charles has decorated an entire wall in his office just with the sales awards and plaques that Steve has won over the years.

"I call it the Lord Jesus' wall," says Steve, "even when my clients are not believers and don't understand it! Whenever I get a new award, I hang it up here as a trophy for God so that He gets the glory."

Steve says that he has learned to take the Caleb anointing right into negotiations with potential buyers. "To go after clients and orders we need a spirit of obedience and faith," he says. "These are the giants in our land." Since he started doing this, the orders are getting larger and larger—and so are the commission checks!

"When I stop praying and giving God the glory," says Steve, "things start going downhill right away."

Is this a lot of magic and superstition? That's what some people believe. But we never use a prayer principle that isn't right out of the Word of God.

We're using and applying the laws of God in our everyday lives. They aren't just for the ministry, but for business, family and every part of life. We need to remind ourselves who we are on the job and extend the rule of God into every sphere of our lives.

Chapter 9

Travailing in the Spirit

*Thus says the Lord of hosts, "Consider and call for
mourning women, that they may come;
and send for skillful wailing women
...that our eyes may run with tears
and our eyelids gush with water."*
—Jeremiah 9:17-18

"Taking the show on the road" meant my waiting was
over. Later I would go deeper into the mysteries of intercession, but for now God knew I needed to test my new
skills in front-line combat.

Revival time had come! The fields were ripe for har-
vesting. My part was to prophetically sound the trumpet,
mobilizing God's people against an unforgiving, relent-
less foe. But the glamour of my early ministry faded to
black as I move out and found how misunderstood
prophecy was in the five-fold ministry.

God spoke, *"I have called only one Moses, one
Mary, one Ezekiel and one Nancy. Go. As I was
with Moses, I will be with you. Go tell the brethren
what I have shared with you and take your place.
I AM sends you."*

God is blowing a trumpet in Zion! He answers the
prayers of His body through His prophets. When He

moves, He first sends those who can hear and proclaim His commands. *"Believe in the Lord your God, and you shall be established; believe His prophets, and you shall prosper,"* promises 2 Chronicles 20:20. That's what we need today, "20/20" vision! The church still needs to recognize those who are called to faithfully sounding the alarm to a world slow to hear.

However, I had a fresh problem. Where would I get a prophetic team to join me for this new ministry? I could not work alone. Without the St. Clair Jesus Circle, I needed a new group of missionary workers, a crusading band who would travel northward.

Carol, still with me, was the cornerstone. She was propelled forward by what God had already revealed. Together, we targeted Mount Pleasant, but there was still no one else on our team.

Besides, I was afraid to trust myself to her.

More Wounds from Trusted Friends

Leading a women's ministry team is quite different than working with men. Ongoing relationships and friendships are more important to us, so it is hard to accept the rejection that often comes with the calling. We are more sensitive to each other and therefore more vulnerable. Because we think symmetrically and relate to each other as equals or peers, I find that women have a much harder time accepting spiritual authority and direction from other women.

Giving direction and accepting rejection were the most painful part of the work for me to accept. After the first few rejections, I was cautious. I learned to hold onto fragile Christian friendships very tenderly, loosely and with much love, since they can be lost in an instant. It's amazing how fast "best girlfriends" separate when one asserts spiritual authority or speaks the truth. That's why I think fewer females are called to become prophets!

My second and third great rejections followed Springfield and extended into the St. Clair years. It was unspeakably painful to have my very closest Christian friends turn against me.

I remember running to the bathroom after one of my first Christian friends let me down in Pleasant Ridge. Like Elijah after his battle with the priests of Baal, there were times when I wanted to slink away to my cave and lick my wounds—feeling sad and lonely, angry at both God and man.

Witchcraft!

One such time of withdrawal followed my second great rejection. Believe it or not, during a women's retreat, I was fingered for being a witch. I was so totally unprepared to handle such a bizarre and outrageous accusation that I went into shock. I took it very personally. All the demons of hell seemed to know that they could torment me gleefully with the memory. It took years to heal.

The story sounds funny now. Then, however, it was a dreadfully serious misunderstanding, a classic example of how mass hysteria can take over when strong leadership is lacking.

The incident began during an extended praise time. The Holy Spirit gave a strange but Spirit-led prophecy. The Lord warned us through me not to focus our attention on the guest speaker, "since she would not always be there." Then the speaker herself confirmed this, exhorting the group to turn their eyes toward Christ and not to human flesh.

So far, so good. The Lord was bringing us an important truth. But then the guest speaker collapsed on the platform in a dead faint. For an instant, the room went silent with paralyzing fear. Before anyone moved, a voice clearly exclaimed, "There's a spirit of witchcraft in the room!"

"Somebody pray!" retorted another very frightened and urgent voice. Panic spread as if a fox had gotten in the hen house.

I was on my feet starting to pray when another woman cut me off. "Not you!" she shouted hysterically.

Then three or four of the women, whom I knew were on the planning committee, came over, surrounded me and asked me to come out with them into the hallway. There, they formed a circle around me to exorcise a demon!

I wanted to laugh, but I realized they were totally serious. Trying to be humble, I submitted to the prayers, occasionally protesting my innocence! "She won't be delivered," declared one of the women, passing a judgment that spread to everyone in minutes.

I was shunned for the rest of the retreat. My roommate moved out! That night I cried alone in my room. Everyone had turned against me. Even my ride home left without me!

The leadership team asked to meet me again, and I expected they would try another deliverance session. But I had already bound everything in me that was not of God and knew that I was not practicing anything occultic. The embarrassed committee realized what a foolish mistake had been made. The badly-handled meeting ended in confusion, without even an apology or closing prayer!

I was naive in the Lord and profoundly wounded that friends could accept or repeat such a silly charge.

The effect of this incident on me was the same as gossip. It ended in broken fellowship. Since no charges were made, no defense could be made. The net result was as bad as if it were true!

A Tragic Misunderstanding

Having cried all the way home, I greeted my husband through puffy eyes and running mascara. "So much for spiritual retreats!" said Charles. "If this is what your friends do to you, I wonder what your enemies are like!"

What's worse, I had already scheduled a luncheon for some of the women of that same group for the next day. Nobody showed up, further building a wall of denial and shame.

I didn't know yet how to seek reconciliation. Out of ignorance, I'm sure, the pastoral leadership of the church did not intervene. As a result, our relationships were never the same.

But God did not leave me comfortless. One saint who saw it all finally called and give me a comforting word from the Lord over the phone: *"You are a woman being rejected by man, but there will come a day when they will know you are anointed. You will be known as a great woman of God."*

"You're Not of God!"

The third great rejection occurred with Sharon Bradley at Springfield Christian Fellowship. I missed them. I continued to give Sharon space to grow by not attending services, but I tried to keep in touch with little cards and phone calls. The calls got shorter. Sharon's answers were abrupt, without a smile in her voice.

My offers of help were rebuffed. Sharon didn't have time anymore even to consider my ideas or listen to suggestions. I wanted to ask about the spiritual progress of old friends, but her answers made my questions seem foolish and improper. Finally, Sharon actually stopped talking with me entirely. We had nothing more to discuss. I had been written off.

Feeling forgotten and left out, I made one last bold attempt to try to force the door back open, which backfired in a most embarrassing way. For years, the memory made me want to sink into the floor every time it came back.

One day, I showed up on Sharon's doorstep unannounced with a carload of friends to attend a meeting. I had built up the Springfield fellowship to my new friends and expected Sharon would welcome visitors. Instead, she was stunned to see us—and very, very defensive.

"Hi, Sharon!" I called with a smile as she appeared in the doorway. "We just came over to join you for the meeting."

Instead of greeting me or moving, Sharon stood in the doorway to deliberately block our entrance. Anger and frustration clouded her face. I could see she was desperate for words. "You're not of God!" she angrily screamed. "Get out! You're not welcome here." With that, Sharon slammed the door shut and loudly banged the dead-bolt into place.

Scarlet-faced, with tears brimming in my eyes, I knocked and knocked, but no one came to the door. Finally, one of the women took my arm and said, "Nancy, let's go. There's nothing you can do now." We walked back to the car in silence, my friends too embarrassed for my sake to talk about it.

And it didn't end there. Sharon must have felt that she had to justify herself, so she began a letter-writing campaign to discredit me with the people who had ordained us both.

Nobody ever warned me of Satan's tricks to divide the body of Christ through power struggles and pride. Backbiting, gossip and doctrinal disputes are the "respectable sins" used to divide Christ's body. Every move of God attracts jealous, self-appointed, theological police who delight in being "right." I just couldn't believe that Sharon would try to join them to discredit me.

Covenant with Carol

Meanwhile, Carol and I were meshing together nicely in the ministry. But I was scared of getting too close, afraid that she might someday reject me as the others had. My open wounds from the first three rejections I had suffered in ministry—with the Billy Graham crusade, on the women's retreat, and from Sharon—were still not healed.

It was wonderful to have a sidekick again, but I wondered constantly if Carol would hold up under the pressure ahead. My mind went back to Diane Ferkel who had also been so strong at the beginning. Then I remembered how she finally reached a point of no return where she had to say "No more!" Would Carol Gibson someday drift away from me like that? Or worse, would she turn on me as Sharon did?

I couldn't seem to release this worry to the Lord. It was always in the back of my mind and hindered the outreach. Finally, I realized that I had to confront her with my feelings, so I jumped in my car and drove 80 miles to her house! "Carol," I began, "I think God is calling us together for now, but I want you to know up front that Jesus is Lord of this ministry. He tells us when to go and when to stop. We can only work together as long as He wants us to do so."

For the next three intense years, Carol and I were a lot more open with our feelings. She went out ministering with me, and we made a great team! In meetings, we practiced mutual submission and blended well together.

In Carol, God had given me another Moses who managed the details and worked hard; serious, but still able to have fun; strong, but teachable. Most of all, she was a great intercessor.

We agreed in prayer and travailed easily together. She was an excellent birthing-partner. God used us wonderfully as a team.

Prophecy Starts in the Womb of Prayer

Carol and I were soon joined by others, including a student activist named Betty. This new group hurled itself into listening, travailing prayer. That's the womb of prophecy from which every move begins. We marched forward on our knees.

Before I took each new step, I always brought my plans into the Holy of Holies before God, seeking His approval. Without His permission and blessing, I dared not move forward.

In this sense, prayer is the first real action in any ministry. God reveals a need. You consider your options. You decide upon a plan. But then you must stop and give birth to a move in the spiritual world before you step out in the physical one.

Only then can you bring forth the word of the Lord, because the word of God is both law and creative force—it is a judgment or decree that must be obeyed. Unless prophecy begins in submissive intercession, the prophet cannot dare to speak the mind of Christ. The word of faith cannot be spoken unless first you have discerned it through waiting upon the Lord in active, listening prayer. That is the secret to all prophetic power.

Getting God's Approval for the Move

Once as I was pray-reading about the general assembly of the firstborn in Hebrews 12:22-28, God gave me a vision about how we receive our blessings and inheritance in the *"kingdom which cannot be shaken"* (v. 28).

I was actually standing in that heavenly parliament with the Lord Jesus. He explained what the general assembly was doing. Right next to us, wearing a gray, pinstriped suit was Abraham.

"Lord," I asked in astonishment, "why is Abraham wearing a suit?"

"He can wear anything he wants up here," replied Christ in a matter-of-fact tone.

God the Father, the Judge of All, was seated at the head of the assembly along with Abraham and saints from all ages. The discussion was about revival on earth.

Christ impressed upon me that plans for revival had to be approved by the assembly. I was amazed. I always thought that God made all the decisions about revivals and moves of His Holy Spirit, but it seems that the whole people of God have a say in it—not just those of us who are praying on earth!

Then the Lord gave me a tablet to read which I couldn't comprehend. He tried to explain it to me, but still I didn't understand. Finally, He told me just to wait. The tablet began to glow red-hot, dissolving into a kind of vapor which was absorbed into my body and spirit.

Next, the Lord presented a scroll to me and instructed me to eat all of it, but it was too hard for me to swallow. To make it easier, Christ divided it into four parts. I ate it while the assembly was dismissed and then waited for them to return in session.

When they reassembled, I presented the information the Lord had given to me. The words came not from mouth, but from my innermost being.

After I had finished, Christ spoke gently to me, *"The program is approved."*

Buying the Deed to Our Inheritance

When Carol and I drove to New York to help bring in revival for all the United States, the Lord revealed to us that the physical world mirrors the spiritual. To cast down idols and bind the ruling spirits is not enough. We must build something in place of these things. As Christ taught, demons abhor empty spaces; they will come back if their places aren't filled.

Building a spiritual house is amazingly similar to building a physical one. Before starting, you need a building permit. And before the permit, you need a deed or lease on the property.

Building our new home with Charles taught me these lessons. Before we could turn over a shovelful of dirt, we had to find the right site and get a clear deed to it. I was fascinated at how complicated it was to purchase the land, clear the title and record our deed, with weeks of waiting at each stage. Finally, we had a right to build.

Exactly the same thing happens in the spiritual world. In Jeremiah 32 is a remarkable story of how God told the prophet to buy property and get a deed to it. At the time, Jeremiah was in prison and seemed to have no personal future. Outside the city walls, the Chaldeans were attacking. King Zedekiah's sons were about to be slain before his eyes, and he would be dragged off to

Babylon. Jerusalem itself would be destroyed. Yet God told Jeremiah to buy land and plan for the future. The message is clear. There was hope for God's people no matter how dark their circumstances seemed.

Nothing is different for us today. God has given us lands and nations to possess for the move of God. There are hidden peoples still without salvation. There are neighborhoods and churches without the move of God, dead as the dry bones in Ezekiel 37.

Foreign visitors, prisoners and hospital patients wait for someone to come and speak a word of faith into their lives and situations. Plus, of course, millions are in bondage to alcohol, drugs, materialism, politics, sex addictions, perversion and entertainment. In the midst of their darkness and death, someone has to come and buy the deed so that they can be set free to plan a future.

Every move of God has a catalyzing Ezekiel, a single individual with an anointed word that brings dry bones to life. Our God is resurrection and life. In His earthly ministry, Christ never met a corpse that He didn't raise from the dead!

That's where we come in. As intercessors and prophets, we have to speak that word and purchase that deed. When I read Jeremiah 32, I asked the Lord, "How can I buy the land and purchase the deed when I don't have any money?"

God spoke, *"You don't need money. Buy it with the Holy Ghost."*

This is the age of grace. We don't have to go to the fearful slopes of Mount Sinai that burned with fire and judgment to purchase the deed. Christ has already paid the price with His blood and poured out the Holy Spirit on us as a down payment on life eternal. We have the purchase price in our hands. We can buy the deed to the next move with the Holy Spirit.

So, I went by faith into the throne room of God and purchased the deed to the land for the move of God. By faith I received it. Now, when the Lord sends me out to possess the land, I have the required deed and authority to occupy it.

Three Critical Questions

Based on these revelations, I made sure that our little team always asked three questions before any ministerial action:

First, have we travailed and given birth to the plan in the Spirit? Are we trying to build something for God that has been conceived by the Holy Spirit? In other words, are we planning to build on holy ground in the will of God?

Second, have we had the blueprints approved in the general assembly of Hebrews 12? You must take your plans before the church triumphant. Does it have the approval of God and His people? Does Scripture agree?

Third, have we been trying to possess the land without buying the deed to it? Has God authorized us to possess it yet?

Running to Arizona

> "Therefore, we also, since we are surrounded by so great a cloud of witnesses, let us lay aside every weight, and the sin which so easily ensnares us, and let us run with endurance the race that is set before us." (Hebrews 12:1)

> "Do you not know that those who run in a race all run, but one receives the prize? Run in such a way that you may obtain it." (1 Corinthians 9:24)

These Scriptures became important commands to us once we emerged from our prayer closets. It isn't enough to just be a Christian activist picketing abortion clinics and witnessing in the streets. It isn't enough to be at the local church every time the door opens. Obedience must extend into the details of the ministry.

When the Lord gave victory commands to Gideon, He paid amazing attention to detail. Look for God in the details. He will show you what He wants next and how He wants it, if you'll let Him. We had to learn this on a practical mission.

One of our first forays after St. Clair was a trip to Arizona. The Lord gave us only the destination—details were to follow! We left without speaking invitations, itinerary, or even financial support! This was a test of submission for all of us.

Leading the mission team was no picnic, although I tried to lighten up whenever I could to let Carol and Betty have some fun. One night we even went to the ballet in Phoenix!

However, one day at lunch, when Carol announced that she needed to buy a stamp for a postcard she had just picked up. I wanted to move on as fast as possible. "Carol," I exhorted, "we're in battle now! Don't look back. You'll get melancholic and homesick. We're not on holiday here. No postcards!"

Silently stewing for awhile, she finally responded poutingly, "You can't say that. I can buy a stamp if I want to—and I do! I'm going to find the post office!" Without waiting for a reply, she jumped for the door.

Finishing our meal, we asked directions for the post office and caught up with her. We arrived in time to see Carol emerge with an angry, puzzled look on her face.

"What's wrong?" I asked.

"They're out of stamps!"

I couldn't believe my ears. A post office that was out of stamps! I resisted the urge to laugh out loud. "Maybe God is trying to say something to us," I said, still trying not to be sarcastic.

But Carol was stubborn. On the way back to the interstate, she saw a souvenir shop with a spinning rack of postcards outside the door. "Pull in here," she cried. "I'm sure they must have stamps."

"Okay," I said, "but this is the last stop!" The car had hardly come to a halt before Carol was out the door. She soon came back with an even more dejected look.

"No stamps?" I asked, trying to keep my poker-face.

"They had stamps in the machine," she replied, "but it took my money, and they got stuck coming out. The stamps are up inside the machine."

Betty and I couldn't hold it in any longer. We laughed until we almost fell off our seats. It seemed that this time, God was having a little fun with us. He just wasn't going to let Carol get away with her tantrum.

Mountaintop Move of God

Go up go up to the mountains, and see what the land is like.   *(Numbers 13:17-18)*

From our intercession times, this Scripture had been given as the theme of this mission to Arizona. We knew from prophetic words that God was leading us to high places where we would find the key to this situation—a lesson we had discovered while in prayer in New York. Like the deed to the land, the Lord had shown me that some doors could only be opened by receiving the key to them in prayer.

God was sending us to Arizona to open doors. When we arrived in Phoenix, the Lord confirmed to us in prayer that this was the destination. However, we didn't see a mountaintop or a high place anywhere.

Remembering that we should always go *"to the Jew first,"* we found a messianic fellowship. They welcomed us, but didn't give us an opportunity to speak. The next day, I had a strong feeling that we should go back.

The rabbi was out, but his wife eagerly welcomed us. We were soon having a great time sharing in the Lord. When she heard about our prayer ministry, she pulled us into the back rooms where they ran a struggling national radio ministry to the Jews. For the next two hours, we went through the studio, praying for everybody and blessing the equipment, the files and every aspect of their broadcasting outreach. Afterwards, a man said we needed to go up on the mountain where the broadcast tower was located.

"What mountain?" we asked in astonishment. "Is there a mountain around here? We've been looking for a mountain!" He drew a map for us. Carol and I rushed to the car, praising God like little children for this miracle breakthrough. What an amazing answer to prayer!

On the mountain crest, we found an even more amazing sight. There were native American religious shrines. In St. Clair, we had prayed about Indians in Arizona! We cursed the animistic shrines and bound the power of evil spirits, loosing the Gospel into all the tribal peoples of Arizona. We turned to pray in every direction of the compass, claiming the whole United States.

Then we shouted out into the valley below, "Jesus is Lord! Jesus is coming again!"

From somewhere down below, an invisible voice responded, "Hallelujah!"

Joyfully, we turned to leave and noticed for the first time the tall broadcasting tower in the distance. Hiking to it, we laid hands on the structure and ecstatically took authority over the airwaves for Christ.

God had answered our prayers and fulfilled the vision we had for an Arizona mountaintop experience. We couldn't have planned it any better. God was in the details. He brought us 2,000 miles for that moment.

Forsaking All to Follow Him

We returned to Michigan, eager to press toward Mount Pleasant and the areas that God showed us under the starburst. I still carried the map that Gail had drawn before her death. It had become a fixation for us.

God spoke, *"Nancy, whosoever comes after Me must forsake all or she cannot be My disciple!"*

"I have, Lord," I replied. "I've not held anything back. What do you want from me? It's yours, Lord."

God answered, *"The map. Your books. Your college transcripts."*

I argued with Him, "Why the map? Doesn't it show us your plan? Why my books? They are all written by good Christian teachers. Why my transcripts? I might need them if I ever return to school for a higher degree."

Then I realized how each of these things had become a little idol in my life. My trust in them was too great. Nothing would stand before God. I made a nice little fire out of them in my backyard.

"Oklahoma, Here We Come!"

God spoke again. *"Nancy, measure My move. Measure the height of it, the breadth of it, the width of it."*

"How, Lord?" I asked.

"Go beyond healings and blessings. Look at what I am doing in the world. See the needs. See the nations as I see them."

"But how?" I repeated.

"Look at what I am doing."

As we started to study the Scriptures on measuring, I found that the Bible had a lot more to say about measuring and keeping track of God than I had realized. The Lord wants us to celebrate His mighty works and wonders, to recall His past miracles and rescues, and to note what He is doing in the present. But we didn't really understand it all until Betty suggested a mission to Oklahoma.

Betty operated under a real apostolic anointing. She was continually starting new groups and organizing fellowships wherever she went. Recently, she had led some Roman Catholics into the Holy Spirit. They were beginning groups around Okeene, Oklahoma.

We took our plan into the general assembly and got it approved. Mount Pleasant would have to wait a little while longer. Soon, we were back on the road again—this time following the Lord to the oil fields of Oklahoma.

Chapter 10

Revival in Mount Pleasant

Behold, I stand at the door and knock. If anyone hears
My voice and opens the door, I will come in to him
and dine with him, and he with Me.
—Revelation 3:20

Oklahoma was a necessary prelude to the Mount Pleasant revival. We needed that trip to be able to understand fully the importance of Zechariah's vision to "measure the move," to pronounce God's will with prophetic authority and power.

In Okeene, Betty Dickson and I were the guests of George and Jerry Kubat. They were renewal leaders in a revival then sweeping the western plains with awesome power. Hundreds of prayer and praise groups were meeting in churches and homes, so we ministered to hungry new believers in the power of God's Word day and night.

George was a consultant to wildcatters, people in the oil business who risk personal fortunes drilling new wells. He traveled extensively, inspecting oil fields and potential drill sites.

"What actually do you do?" I asked one day, my curiosity finally getting the best of me.

"I measure the flow," he said.

My jaw dropped in awe. His words were almost the same as those we had received repeatedly during listening prayer for Mount Pleasant!

Seeing my astonished gaze, he gestured for me to follow, "Let me show you!" Soon, we were driving over the bleak Oklahoma landscape as George pointed out topography he had already surveyed. Later, he took us up close to see how he actually measured the flow at the well head.

Jerry and I giggled at the irony of what we were doing as we walked through the gates of the Grace Oil Field in Okeene. (That's really what it was named!) As George taught us about measuring oil, we realized that the Lord was actually giving us a lesson in measuring grace for end-times revival!

"You see," he explained as we climbed an oil rig, "my job is to visit each of these wells and check the depth and flow rate. Monitoring it over time, we can estimate the life of the field. By combining all this with the topography, I can predict where the flow is going—even where to drill and not drill wells!"

Jerry and I rolled our eyes at each other in amazement. God was showing us an incredible real-life parallel to what He had already called us to do. Just as the prophet Zechariah envisioned the measurement of the move of God in His day, we needed to measure the move in ours!

Measuring the Move

We first came across this mysterious instruction while pray-reading Zechariah. Learning to measure the move of God changed my whole ministry. That's how I begin to exercise authority in declaring the prophetic word.

Measuring through listening prayer is really the first step in prophetic ministry. If we can't say, "Thus saith the Lord," then we are no longer prophets! There is no way we can pronounce God's will unless we've discerned God's clear leading. We can accept nothing less than God's true word! Such presumption would bring disgrace and ridicule.

This separates the prophet from the pastor, from the teacher and from the rest of the five-fold ministry. A preacher delivers a homily. A teacher presents a lesson. But the prophet pronounces a verdict or judgment. He delivers an order from the throne of God. We issue commands that almighty God is going to enforce with His irresistible will.

The Lord was showing me that prophecy is much more than delivering a nice thought from the Bible. It means delivering the very word of God with power that comes from an intimate knowledge of the holy! And it can often be mixed with spiritual gifts like healing, knowledge or wisdom.

Three Elements in Prophecy

This concept differs from the common Bible teaching which limits prophecy to only two elements, forth-telling and foretelling. The prophet either speaks the mind of God on something (i.e., preaches from Scripture) or forecasts a future event (declares the judgment of God on a matter).

However, real prophesy includes a third vital element: it also creates! The living Word of God is dynamite in the mouth of the prophet. The Word of God does not return empty, but actively accomplishes what God has intended. (See Isaiah 55:11.) This makes prophecy a power gift!

Life-giving Word

God asked the prophet Ezekiel, *"Can these bones live?"* Ezekiel looked at those dry, separated, scattered bones and there wasn't much faith in his tentative answer. *"Oh, Lord God,"* he dodged, *"You know"* (Ezekiel 37:3).

But God wouldn't let his prophet get away with a wimpy reply like that! He wanted to show Ezekiel, and us, the power of the prophetic word to bring life to death, flesh out dry bones, and resuscitate corpses. There is resurrection power in the prophet's tongue.

God ordered Ezekiel, *"Prophesy to these bones, and say to them, 'O dry bones, hear the word of the Lord!'"* (Ezekiel 37:4). He was commanded to give three separate prophecies bringing body, soul and spirit together again. He restored life through the living word of the Lord!

Sometimes, the prophet's tongue works the other way, too. It can bring death, destruction and ruin. The tongue of the prophet is a sword in the hand of God. *"Sharper than any two-edged sword,"* it is capable of cutting apart soul and spirit says Hebrews 4:12.

Armed and Dangerous

The prophet's word is the sword of the spirit, an offensive weapon. He has no kingdom, wealth or force other than the Word of the Lord. And we're no good to God if we leave it in the sheath! We have to use the Word of God actively in every prophetic action, both creating and destroying.

Revelation portrays the Lord Jesus Christ Himself returning with the power of the prophetic word as a destructive weapon:

And out of His mouth went a sharp, two-edged sword.
(Revelation 1:16)

These things says He who has the sharp two-edged
sword. *(Revelation 2:12)*

Repent, or else I will come...quickly, and will fight
against them with the sword of My mouth.
(Revelation 2:16)

Now out of His mouth goes a sharp sword, that with
it He should strike the nations...He Himself treads the
winepress of the fierceness and wrath of Almighty
God. *(Revelation 19:15)*

The Lord showed us that we could not possibly win
against the enemy in Mount Pleasant unless we were
able to address every enemy with, "Thus saith the Lord."
Circumstances, sins and situations which are outside the
will of God must yield to the authority of God's will made
manifest through the mouths of His prophets.

If we understand our ministries, we will see that the
prayer warrior and the prophet are also servants of the
sword, the ones called of God to speak the word of truth
and faith. Salvation, deliverance, renewal, restoration,
healing and judgment—these are all in the move of God
like seeds in an apple. Life and death, curses and blessings, success and failure are all wrapped up in the
prophet's trumpet call!

Flowing in the Anointing

It is no wonder that God-fearing folks tremble at a
real prophet's presence. Genuine prophecy is somewhat
unsettling. We appear on the stage of human history to
cast down and raise up, bind and loose—all in the name

of the living God. Prophecy comes down from God *"who gives life to the dead and calls those things which do not exist as though they did"* (Romans 4:17).

With this power in our tongues, we dare not run ahead of God. Submission is a prime virtue in prophetic ministry. It is why we must humbly measure the move before we speak His commands.

The test of obedience comes repeatedly in the school of the prophets until we learn the habit and attitude of submission! The test of waiting also comes again and again until we yield our natural abilities and strengths to Him.

"Thine is...the power" (Matthew 6:13 KJV) becomes our daily prayer of surrender. The prophet handles God's power like a banker handles money—it may go through his or her hands, but it dare not stick. That's why self-reliance is our greatest enemy in this work and why failure to measure the move is so deadly.

The Lord Jesus spent vast amounts of time in private dialogue with God, earnestly making sure He was always speaking in submission to His Father's will. *"For I have not spoken of My own authority,"* said the Lord Jesus, *"but the Father who sent Me gave Me a command, what I should say and what I should speak"* (John 12:49).

Dare we do less than Christ? He has set the example for us by modeling the perfect prophetic prayer life.

A Lydia for Mount Pleasant

Before Mount Pleasant could explode in revival, Carol and I still needed an open door. There always needs to be a Lydia or a Rahab when a new work starts —someone on the inside who will either open the door or at least leave it unlocked, someone who will hang out a red cord.

Betty Dickson was the door-opener for us at Central Michigan University. When we started, we didn't know a single pastor or student at CMU, the main "industry" in Mount Pleasant. There was no one to issue a Macedonian call to us!

We actually met our Lydia in downtown Detroit! An Afro-American group invited Carol and me to come and explain the current move of God to them.

In the audience was a brilliant but skeptical graduate student. I had never met her before, so neither of us had ever talked about our personal callings or leadings from God. She knew nothing of my interest in Mount Pleasant or CMU. I didn't know that she was a student there. Nor did I know that she was struggling hard to hold together a campus Christian fellowship!

She was facing fierce opposition from black nationalists who opposed evangelism on campus. In fact, the resistance was so intense that she was ready to quit.

As I preached, the Holy Spirit drew me to Betty. She felt the same quickening, but tested me. "If this woman is really of God," she muttered to herself, "she'll give me the right prophecy tonight about what I should do in Mount Pleasant."

I knew nothing about her problem, so the prophecy I was about to give was truly miraculous. When the Holy Spirit came over me, I went directly to where she was sitting with a powerful word of knowledge: *"You must do what God told you to do, and don't let man stop you!"*

That was it. She knew God had spoken directly to her situation. She came forward for the laying on of hands when I gave an invitation. Afterwards, she asked if I would speak to her student group in Mount Pleasant!

Eventually she entered into a prayer covenant with Carol and me, leading us to Oklahoma where we learned to measure the move of God together. Betty prayed with us to locate much *"dry and thirsty"* (Psalm 63:1) human soil that Jesus wanted for His own possession. She was the miracle link coupling me with many young collegians He longed to save.

Before long, we were a familiar trio on campus—Betty, Carol and myself. We networked from one student group to another, using the Big Boy Restaurant as our base of field operations.

The Move Breaks Out!

One breath-taking fall day, the campus was already covered with an ankle-deep carpet of falling leaves, yet the huge maples and elms still had foliage left to form a magnificent canopy over University Avenue. Searching up and down the street for Betty, I felt like I was walking through a cathedral. The trees were at least 60 or 70 feet tall.

The students hurried underneath the arches of red, yellow and gold—rushing between classes, meals and a full evening of study and play. The autumn air crackled with the energies and passions of these beautiful, intelligent young people. Suddenly I felt very much like the middle-aged mother of three teenagers that I was.

Somehow, Betty and I became separated as we witnessed one-on-one. I stopped at His House Christian Fellowship to see if she had gone there. The huge wooden dorm had white pillars and an old-fashioned porch across the front. A brown and white bungalow, it had been framed nearly 100 years ago from northwood timber. Three stories high with plenty of rooms, it was built when CMU was still a "normal college," preparing teachers for one-room country schools.

Recently, Gary Hoss had bought it as a center for campus outreach. He was a local minister with a vision for reaching college students. His House was then a Christian men's residence and study center.

I talked with one of the staff workers who knew Betty, but he hadn't seen her. "Until you find Betty," he suggested, "why don't you wait here?" Gratefully, I lingered on the porch. There was a strong presence of the Holy Spirit.

Since we were all Christians, I found it easy to talk about the vision God was giving us for a revival on campus. The boys began to cluster around me. Soon, I found myself spontaneously preaching and sharing my testimony.

God spoke, *"Tell them about My Holy Spirit."*

"Lord," I argued, "I don't even know these people. They might think I'm a Pentecostal fanatic. Shouldn't I work up to the baptism of Your power slowly?"

"Tell them about My Holy Spirit now."

The boys eagerly listened as I explained how simple it was to receive the baptism in the Holy Spirit—by faith alone, in the same way that you accept your salvation. "It is all of God's grace," I said. "This power for service and holiness is freely available to whoever asks for it, a gift from Christ."

The explanation was barely out of my mouth when the power of God rushed over the group. We stumbled inside for a little more privacy. The living room did not contain much furniture, which was perfect for ministering the Holy Spirit. Within seconds, several of the young men were stretched out on the bare wooden floor in ecstatic prayer.

Tongues of flame seemed to have fallen on the group. Some just knelt in corners and wept. Others sat dazed in worship. Several began prophesying and describing visions. The presence of God was so real that no one could remain standing.

I later learned that these manifestations of the Holy Spirit were not learned responses, but totally spontaneous expressions of God's power. These young men had never before manifested the presence of God like this. Such Spirit-inspired words and actions were a totally new experience for them.

The revival had started without any of the trappings one associates with organized outreach. We had no speakers, no rented halls, no music, no whipped up emotionalism. God had sovereignly moved where and how He wanted without any special preparations except for months of intercession.

God's Offensive Word

But I quickly experienced my first opposition—not from the world, but from other believers! There will always be scribes and Pharisees among us who will be just as offended today as they were when our Lord spoke the creative word which raised Lazarus from the dead. Christ found that even when He spoke with miracle-working power and did undeniable good, some religious leaders still hated Him for it!

In fact, the prophetic word which raised Lazarus from the dead was the one most fatal to Christ. It did more to bring about the crucifixion than any other single event in His ministry! It so upset the power-base of certain Bible teachers in Jerusalem that they plotted His murder from that day forward!

Enter the Sadducees

While the Pharisees attacked Jesus for being "unbiblical" and acting outside their interpretations of Scripture, the Sadducees were offended that Jesus would not submit to their authority and power. Controlling Christians are easily offended by the Holy Spirit. The natural emotions released by any real move of God are scary to those who focus only on the gifts of administration and government.

At Central Michigan, Ken Bell was the student leader in charge of His House Fellowship Center. When he walked in to find revival was sweeping through, he reacted like a typical Sadducee. Ken looked at the living room in horror. At that moment I think he would have preferred to see an orgy instead of the power of God moving with signs and wonders.

Students were praying and worshipping spontaneously. There was shouting, intercession, prophesy, singing, strange tongues, weeping. Some were prophesying to the walls. One young man was stretched out on the floor in ecstatic worship, receiving ministry from the Holy Spirit.

Ken spotted me immediately. "I'm sorry," he said abruptly, "you'll have to go right now. We're supposed to be having dinner.

"Well, I'm sorry, too," I replied. "God is moving, and we're not going until He says go."

Ken turned on his heels and fled to the kitchen. Some of the students moved to their rooms to continue praying. Some went to the kitchen and the dining hall. Others stayed on praying with us.

Still angry, Ken returned in a few minutes, even more worked up and distraught. "Out! Out!" he shouted. "You have to get out. We're eating now."

Betty and I helped the young man on the floor to his feet and temporarily retreated. We were already scheduled to attend a ministerial meeting that night, but we knew the Lord wanted us to return later—and we did.

The revival was just beginning. I was determined that no man would stop it now. I didn't know how to handle Ken, but I did know this was a classic case of obeying God or man. Like the Apostle Peter, I didn't have to think about it. I was obeying God.

Midnight Outpouring

Around 9:00 PM, Carol, Betty and I returned to a girls dorm close to His Place. Ken Bell was nowhere to be seen, so the three of us joined with the women's prayer group that had by now received the revival spirit, too.

Although we didn't know it yet, the revival was spreading from one room to the next all across campus. As each student received the power of God, he or she became a witness, carrying the Spirit to another friend. The result was a number of small prayer meetings with just three or four students in each, many going on simultaneously in different rooms and dorms. In His House, prayer groups were meeting on every floor.

Around 11:00 PM, one of the students came to me breathlessly, "Ken wants to see you!"

"Oh, all right!" I answered, thinking the worst. I imagined that he wanted to reprimand me again and forbid future visits. I hesitated for awhile. This was one of the greatest moves of God I had ever seen, and I didn't want to pull myself away from the presence of God.

After years of daytime ministry to housewives and mothers, seeing God move among young men and women was so exciting. I was thrilled to see this youthful energy being released for God.

Their prayers were different. These were not the "bless me, heal me" cries of homemakers. They were mission-minded and activistic. They named countries I had never heard of and described visions of unreached people finding the Lord. In one of the visions, I saw myself in an arena surrounded by thousands of people in national dress from many tribes, tongues and nations.

Just then another student came upstairs. "Mrs. Milsk, Ken wants to see you. He's waiting to come up."

It was midnight now, time for the third shift to begin in the Detroit automotive plants. I thought of the workers pouring through the gates with their lunch pails. "Well, Carol," I said, "we're going overtime into the third shift!" We had been ministering nearly eighteen hours already, but we felt as fresh as when we started. Very reluctantly, we excused ourselves.

Mother in Israel

It was dark and quiet outside when Ken Bell walked up the sidewalk to the old house where we were praying with the girls. As Ken climbed to the third floor where we were meeting in a large garret prayer-chapel, I could not help laughing at myself. Here I was, a mother of three kids, struggling up and down three flights of stairs on a college campus in the middle of the night.

I was totally out of my league, but grateful to God for choosing me to minister to students young enough to be my children. I was 36 when I came to Christ and discovered the power of God. These college kids were experiencing the fullness of God at 18 or 19 years of age!

The Holy Spirit had broken down all the age and cultural barriers that separated us from these students. God will use any willing vessel. No one questioned our right to be on campus, our age, our gender, our races.

The Holy Spirit gave us favor and acceptance with these teenagers. Our words were attractive and life changing.

Suddenly, I felt like *"a mother in Israel"* (Judges 5:7) to a whole new generation of believers. I could see that their decisions for Christ would affect careers, lives and marriages even after my time on this earth was over.

God had sent us. Fear departed. I welcomed this chance to fellowship with Ken. Suddenly the Holy Spirit flooded me with love for him, and the dreadful sense of confrontation completely disappeared.

"I Want It, Too!"

Instead of the angry scolding I expected, Ken spoke gently. He was quiet and broken. What happened in the next few minutes changed the course of our ministry on campus and began a friendship in ministry with Ken that is still strong today.

Here was a religious leader like Nicodemus, who came to Jesus by night for fear of losing face. "I need to see you about two things," began Ken. "First, I want you to forgive me for throwing you out of His Place Fellowship House tonight. Second, I want that same power of God in my life that I am seeing others receive. Will you lay hands on me for the baptism in the Spirit?"

Ken was the first of many student leaders, chaplains, ministers and pastors in Mount Pleasant who discovered the power of God in a new way during that revival. Others emerged who are still in the ministry as a result.

Sustaining Revival

The Mount Pleasant move lasted for at least two years and is still being felt today. The first secret of sustaining a revival is simply to stay obedient and yielded, to keep on measuring the move and follow it wherever it leads.

"I am the vine, you are the branches," explained Christ in John 15:5. Revival is vine-life in action, staying attached to the branch rather than trying to grow on your own.

Our theme verse for the revival became my life verse, *"As many as are led by the Spirit of God, these are the sons of God"* (Romans 8:14). As a result of following His leading, a number of student-led Christian groups were organized on campus. Students found Christ in almost every meeting.

Just when we thought the move was over, another spurt of growth occurred as another cell was formed. This is the way our Lord predicted His kingdom would grow and penetrate the world.

The second secret of sustaining revival is refusing to let sectarian interests hijack the move. Nothing grieves the heart of God more than when people use His kingdom move to build their own personal kingdoms.

Churches and Christians in the community opened their homes for student Bible studies and discipleship, not trying to hold onto the fruit for themselves. We crossed all denominational and doctrinal lines, sharing Christ without proselytism.

Closed Chapel Opens

Diane Jackson was the official campus chaplain at the ecumenical chapel, and the last religious authority to surrender to what God was doing. Everything about the chapel and her ministry was still entrapped in the latest "radical-chic" theology of the day.

An inner-city Afro-American from a mainline seminary, Diane had to climb over some pretty high walls of prejudice to accept ministry from white, suburban laywomen! Throughout most of the revival, she cautiously held back, but we could see that she was sincerely interested in the phenomenal activity of God's Holy Spirit among the students.

Several of the regular chapel students were attending our home prayer meetings in nearby Coleman, finding deliverance from bondage to sin and fresh power from God. However, because the chapel was the center of established religion on campus, I had never even tried to hold meetings there.

But God was working in Diane's heart. The day finally came when she approached us to ask if we would hold what she called "charismatic" services in the chapel. Diane did all the set-up for the meetings and invited the most liberal Christian students and seminarians. Much to her surprise, and ours, these young people from old-line, traditional, religious families were as eager as the others to receive the infilling of the Holy Spirit.

God moved powerfully. The Lord sent a spirit of humility, and an unquestioning obedience to His commands was pervasive. The men and women would sing and prophesy as God revealed the next step. Many gave up occult objects and personal idols and destroyed unclean posters as a result of those meetings.

"I felt like that onion you talked about," said one girl afterwards. "The Lord was just peeling away my layers of sin and rebellion like skin from an onion."

Fighting for Baptism Rights

But it wasn't always easy. I remember one night we were holding a student meeting in the private home of a

Christian lady near His Place Fellowship House. Into the Bible study walked a strange student, right off the street. Everything about his dress, body language and speech seemed utterly rebellious against all authority. His presence was disturbing.

God spoke, *"Nancy, I have chosen this boy as My own. Bring him to Me tonight and baptize him into My church."*

Not only did this boy seem a million miles from baptism, but I couldn't even imagine him getting saved! As I preached, everything about his face and posture seemed to say "no way!" He was so indifferent that I had a hard time imagining why he even sat through the study. But near the end of the meeting, I issued a salvation invitation. To my amazement, and everyone else's in the room, this boy immediately fell on his knees and publicly invited Christ into his life!

God spoke again, *"Okay, Nancy, take him all the way tonight!"*

"But, Lord," I countered, "this boy has had no instruction. Shouldn't we take some time to disciple him first?"

"You will never see him again. Baptize him into My body tonight."

"Well," I spoke out as firmly as I could, "the Lord is telling me to bring this young man all the way tonight. Where can we baptize him?"

"It's late," argued the hostess, "and we have no place to baptize here. Can't we plan it for another time?" There were other excuses and objections. I could feel a negative wall of resistance growing stronger in the room.

Pulling myself up to full height, I felt the Holy Spirit come over me with great power and boldness. Usually, I am the kind that would give in to the feelings of a group, but there was no doubt that I had heard God.

Obey the Lord Now!

"No!" I almost shouted. "God is saying that we must baptize him now!"

"He can come over to my place," volunteered Pat Neuman, a woman student. So we all went over to her place, filled up the bathtub, and baptized Bill Williams around 10:00 PM.

At that moment the Holy Spirit visited the room in an unforgettable way. The young man was powerfully baptized in the Holy Spirit just as in Acts 19:5-6. No one argued now that we shouldn't have taken this student through the whole salvation experience in a single night. God Himself was stamping His seal of approval on the entire process.

The Miracle of Spiritual Birth

At that moment, all of us felt the same excitement you feel when watching your first childbirth. The spiritual drama unfolded as grace after grace was poured out on this young man.

It was just as if the book of Acts had never ended. This was primitive, simple Christianity as practiced in the homes of the first believers. I could feel the saints of all the ages witnessing what was happening. The evening was authentic and life changing, not only for Bill Williams, but for each one of us who had shared in the birthing process.

"Nancy," said God, *"Don't let them go home without remembering Me in holy communion!"*

"Before Bill leaves our fellowship tonight," I announced, "the Lord would like to have us all join with Him and our brand new brother in holy communion!"

Pat found some bread and grape juice for the eucharistic feast. Soon this young rebel was completing his initiation into Christ's living body by sharing with us in the sacred mysteries!

"Take, eat, this is My body which is broken for you. Do this in remembrance of Me," I said, quoting Christ as I distributed the bread.

"Drink this, all of you; for this is My blood of the new covenant, which is shed for you, and for many, for the remission of sins. Do this, as often as you shall drink it, in remembrance of Me."

The Mount Pleasant revival was still a prelude to God's greatest move, a final global harvest before His return. To learn about it, we had to lay aside the work again and measure the next move. We moved camp to nearby Coleman and prepared for another extended time of waiting on God in the Holy of Holies.

Part Three:

"To the End of the Earth"

*But you shall receive power when the Holy Spirit has come upon you; and you shall be witnesses to Me in Jerusalem, and in all Judea and Samaria, and **to the end of the earth.***
—*Acts 1:8*

The nations are Christ's ultimate desire, the passion of the One who already is "the desire of all nations." Jesus Christ is now calling His people to one last, massive worldwide movement of obedience.

As Nancy responded to God's call, she learned to think globally and act locally, using the anointing that Caleb had to motivate her intercession and her actions. She established an end-times prayer fellowship that clearly comprehended the mind and heart of the Lord not only for the local community, but for the entire world. As the intercessory group learned to hear the voice of God and proclaim His will, the ministry spread *"to the end of the earth."*

Nancy offers you the same ability to become an overcomer in this last chapter of human history, a chapter whose Author has already put pen to paper.

Chapter 11

Michigan: Spiritual Command Center

*Now when the Day of Pentecost had fully come, they were
all with one accord in one place.*
—Acts 2:1

Our Mount Pleasant ministry usually began and ended
with prayer meetings in nearby Coleman, Michigan.
Often students and pastors from the revival joined us.
Gradually the times of prayer grew into day-long events.

The Lord was calling us apart again for an extended
time of listening prayer and revelation. Immanuel had a
fresh vision and word for us. I felt pregnant again in my
spirit. Where would this new preparation lead us? Michigan seemed complete.

God works in seasons, dry and rainy times. However,
waiting is the norm—the wilderness before the promised
land, deserts before gardens. This is God's way with us.

The years of waiting in Coleman were by no means
unpleasant. The Mt. Pleasant revival simply continued
in another form, turning inward as God called us deep
into Himself to accept His commands for the next step.

Carol Gibson joined Bonnie and Melvin Cozat to
form the core of this new circle. Betty Dickson and a

growing fellowship of local townsfolk who looked upon Bonnie as their overseer usually met with us.

From the first, the Coleman prayer meetings focused not only on the local community, but regions beyond as well. We didn't understand spiritual warfare yet, but we were actually gathering a war council together.

Leadership Plan Revealed

Early on, the Lord gave a vision for the Coleman ministry as a spinning wheel with five spokes. Each spoke represented one of the five-fold ministries of Ephesians 4:11. In the vision, each became active in turn as the wheel rotated. God wanted to show us His pattern in miniature for the church. No one ministry dominated. Apostle, prophet, pastor, teacher and evangelist each edified the body for outreach.

We sometimes lost all track of time. Once we waited on the Lord for three straight days without leaving the house. Our group literally wore out the living room carpet with our knees!

Then a prophecy came forth that showed us the future purpose for the meeting. The Lord said, *"Nancy, you will be training My handmaidens for worldwide outreach. You will go for My sake to ambassadors, kings and bishops. You will go to many nations, peoples and lands."*

This was clearly a prophecy for international ministry. From Coleman, we were going to touch the world —not just Michigan, or even just the United States! God was getting us ready for global missionary outreach.

Later, an almost identical prophecy confirmed this word during a Nora Lam breakfast in Detroit. After that, the same message came many times in many places. The Holy Spirit was reserving me for international revival.

The vision of this revival was multi-racial, multi-cultural and multi-denominational. It networked the whole body of Christ together regardless of gender, color or doctrine. The Lord wants to orchestrate His people in an end-times song of service.

Nancy, Take Your Place!

As the Chief Cornerstone called us deeper into Himself, I found the Holy Spirit leading through me with bold, new authority. We started going into the Holy of Holies almost immediately after the group gathered. Sometimes we would just walk into the living room and collapse under the power of God. This sense of holy presence didn't need to be worked up.

It was a special time. Robed in the righteousness of Christ according to Psalm 118:19-29, I found again that holiness is irresistible to God. We seemed to have immediate access to the King of Kings.

Some of this righteousness had to do with the holiness of the place. Bonnie kept a spotless house. Like her life, it was dedicated wholly to the Lord's service, a real retreat center in every sense of the word. Even today, I love to go there to get away from worldly pressures and focus on the Lord.

Carol Looks Back

As the weeks of waiting stretched into months, Carol let us know she was not ready for a return to intense intercession. She resisted this new, simpler intimacy. Sometimes she would contradict me openly.

Our years of mobile ministry together used her strengths as an activist, administrator and leader. Now humility and sanctification were the order of the day. The Lord was slowly forming new strength within us as He forms stalagmites underground, one drop of water at a time.

Once when the Spirit overshadowed me, I blew a sound from my mouth like a trumpet. The rival spirit of Miriam came over Carol. "I can blow the trumpet, too!" she shouted perversely, imitating the sound of my voice. Her flesh was struggling for power and attention.

Another time, the Lord commanded me to eat the scroll and receive the Word of God in my inner being. "I can eat the scroll, too!" she challenged.

This childish envy grew so strong that sometimes she couldn't bear to sit in our circle. I started to notice her empty chair when we met as a group.

When she did come, she was so distracting I had to directly command her to listen to the Word. Once, I saw a strange look come over her face, a hideous look of self-determination.

"Rebellion!" pronounced the Lord.

"Oh, no, God!" I cried, "Not the spirit of rebellion, not in my dear friend, Carol! She's been so good for me, Lord."

"Rebellion!" repeated the Lord.

The revelation panicked me. I actually argued with the Lord in her defense. I didn't want this word of knowledge. I tried to get God to retract His judgment! I knew that rebellion from Carol meant the end of our relationship, and I didn't want that.

Why would a trusted co-worker turn against me after all we had been through together? I finally agreed with God that she really did have the spirit of rebellion, which the Bible says is as bad as witchcraft.

Yet, I couldn't bring myself to deliver the word of the Lord to her. I was too personally attached. Deeply hurt, I kept the revelation to myself.

However Bonnie and Melvin noticed the new tension in our group. They soon got me alone, rebuking me in love. "Nancy, would you take your place?" Bonnie almost shouted at me. "Quit letting people like Carol walk all over you."

Bonnie was acting as the pastor to our little group. To have a pastor urge you to give leadership is a wonderful invitation for any prophet. The five-fold ministry was really working.

I thanked God for giving our group an overseer who had the humility and wisdom to welcome a prophet. *"He who receives a prophet in the name of a prophet shall receive a prophet's reward"* (Matthew 10:41).

Appointed Leadership

From that day forward, I began freely exercising my spiritual authority in the Coleman group. Bonnie's exhortation reminded me again that I really was called to this ministry by name. I needed to accept that call and take my place without apology as so many had prophesied to me. Not to speak was disobedience.

My lack of theological degrees, seminary education and acceptance by male clergy was not the issue. What did it matter if I, a woman, ministered mostly from the pews? Bonnie helped me to see the reality of God's call on my life and to look not on the outward things, but on the inner things of the heart. Obedience was all that really mattered to God.

From then on, I took charge without apology, helping other women discover their gifts, minister in turn and pray in order. Bonnie set the example by yielding frequently to my leadership. Soon we were functioning as a real New Testament church.

That was too much for Carol! When she saw the holy order that was emerging, the spirit of rebellion took over. She fled the regular fellowship of our group and tried to start her own ministry. This time, instead of clinging to her and trying to persuade her to come back like I would have done in the past, I accepted this split as from the Lord.

"Let her go," said the Lord. *"She has a work to do, and you have a work to do."*

I realized that her work in my ministry was much like Judas' in the ministry of Christ! Our Lord knew that Judas was going to betray Him, but never purged him from the group. In fact, he kept him in a position of power and trust as treasurer of the band. He seemed willing to sit back and let Judas play out his hand. I decided to handle Carol in the same way.

Yet, "sin is its own reward." Never is this old proverb more true than for a person choosing to continue in rebellion. "I feel like God has abandoned me," she confessed one day as we talked. Carol took herself outside our fellowship and the wonderful move of God that we were seeing, but it was a choice she had made.

Good-bye, Fear of Rejection

This fifth rejection was a critical turning point in my ministerial relationships with other people. I finally realized that sometimes I just have to let people go their own way.

This is never easy. It hurts, but it hurts God even more. We are sharing in the sufferings of Christ when we are rejected for His sake. His bloody sacrifice on the cross is being rejected.

Imagine how Christ felt when He had to watch as the rich young ruler *"went away sorrowful"* (Matthew 19:22). Our tendency would be to run after the youth to plead with him and give him another chance. But that is not God's way. While He is longsuffering, forgiving and merciful, He never tampers with a person's free will. He never compromises the terms of discipleship.

A prophet has the same obligation. You have the power of attorney for God. You must deliver the message the Lord lays on you, accepting the consequences, and stay on as long as He asks you to wait. However, when He says go, you must be willing to walk away without looking back!

Part of learning maturity in Christian service is learning how to make graceful and gentle exits, ones that don't leave open wounds or ugly scars. Like evangelists, prophets have to learn how to keep their spiritual bags packed.

We aren't high-pressure salesmen for God. It is not our job to cajole, compromise, negotiate or beg people to get right with God. Not everyone wants to hear God, even those who say they do. King Zedekiah in Jeremiah 37 is a striking example. Many are caught up in pride, secret sins and hidden idolatry. They end up rejecting God's word and the prophet who brings it!

Coleman helped me to grow comfortable with the rejection part of my ministry. I learned to deliver the word without feeling guilt when I lost a friend or a relationship.

God's Faithful Receive the Word!

A real prophet is not afraid to bring the pure Word of the Lord because truth will always win a hearing among God's faithful ones. It separates the true believers from the false.

As I boldly proclaimed God's mind through words of knowledge and wisdom, prophecies and revelations, we developed into a group who witnessed God moving in prophecy. We wanted more. The question and heart-attitude that characterized our little group of seekers was, "What will God show us next?"

This expectancy blessed them because God filled their hungry hearts. It blessed me, too, because it provoked in me the kind of holy boldness I would need for my upcoming international ministry. Each week we experienced more revival and revelation. Many secrets unfolded.

Body Life and Unity

The first thing God showed me was the secret of unity. God spoke, *"Nancy, make a covenant with Me for the unity of the whole body of Christ. Don't ask the believers to covenant with you. Instead, you covenant with Me, and I'll bring them to you."*

In the Holy of Holies, the Father, Son and Holy Spirit are continually submitting to one another in absolute harmony. As we submit to God, we automatically enter into this harmony with the Trinity and into another harmony with other believers who are also submitting themselves at the same time!

Unity is a grace gift from God. It is not something we can mandate through associations, councils, creeds, denominations, pledges, statements of faith or vows. Actually, these attempts divide Christ's body even more!

We cried out for the reality of Philippians 2:2-5 to come into the room, that we might be *"...like-minded, having the same love, being of one accord, of one mind. Let nothing be done through selfish ambition or conceit, but in lowliness of mind let each esteem others better than himself...Let this mind be in you which was also in Christ Jesus."* We prayed that we might *"do all things without murmuring and disputing"* (v. 14).

I found that the move of God came so easily when we were empty of such sinful divisions. Yet, I could not wish them away. Praying, preaching and scolding didn't work either! The sin of disunity seems to be a contagious disease in our churches, as well as families, races, nations and every other human institution.

As we fell at the foot of the cross and exalted Christ together in praise and worship, unity manifested itself as a free gift. With unity always comes the move of God!

At the End of the Pew

The second lesson I had to learn was the secret of contentment. Occasionally, we would have a visiting evangelist, missionary or pastor speak. When we did, we would take up a little collection to bless them financially.

This began to get under my skin. "Lord," I cried, "I drive hours to get up here, and I've been coming for years. Why don't they ever think of an offering for me? Don't I deserve double honor for all my work and expenses?"

God spoke bluntly, *"What do you want, My power or the money?"*

In an instant, I saw clearly that it was that simple a choice. I could continue to preach from the pews and be used of God to usher in revival, or I could seek the symbols of human status. If I opted for the second choice, that's all I would get—mere offerings, puny titles and fleeting prestige.

I fell on my knees and cried out to God in repentance, "Lord, you know I want Your power first, foremost and always! I want to flow in Your flow and move in Your move. I want the blessing of God and nothing less!"

"Nancy," Gail had prophesied to me years before, "God has called you to lead a spiritual SWAT team. Don't seek to be exalted and lifted up. Be content to minister from the end of the pew, to speak off the wall. You don't need the glory of men or the money to do what God has called you to do!"

The Authority Question

Next, I learned the secrets of getting beyond gender. This is not really a problem to me anymore. I don't feel limited in my ministry because I am a woman.

Occasionally, I find a man who has a strong enough ego to seek the Lord's blessing from me. Once during a wedding, a Roman Catholic priest invited me into a side room. There, I was stunned when he fell on his knees and asked for the Caleb anointing in his ministry! He had read my newsletter prophecies and wanted more power from God.

But this kind of ministry to men is rare—and almost never public. That's sad. Our churches are impoverished because sisters in Christ are too often expected to remain passive, silent recipients instead of sharing their gifts and graces with the whole body.

So I worked to include men in our group, starting with Melvin and the local pastors. We almost always had some men with us.

However, when leading listening-prayer times, I deferred to women and men equally, letting God speak through them both. Some men unconsciously rejected this and drifted away after a couple meetings, but I felt it was essential that we let everyone share. As a result, God worked tremendously through women in our sessions.

At first, my heart grieved over the fact that it seemed so hard to keep men in the circle. God's word is for the whole body of Christ. It bothered me that intercession and prophecy were being relegated to women's meetings.

I joked that we should be called "Deborah's Band" because so much of our intercession energy was being focused on pushing men into position for work. But then I began to see that it was working! We women had the freedom and time to pray, and God was answering our prayers. We were asking the Lord of the harvest to send forth laborers as He had commanded us to pray. In answer to our prayers, God was sending men out. Even if the men didn't recognize us or our ministry, it was being validated week after week.

When I had a message for a male leader, I found that I didn't have to deliver it in a prayer meeting. When I have a specific message or blessing to give, I have learned to call men on the phone or go privately to them. I can deliver the word in the course of a normal conversation just as easily as in a meeting—and often more effectively.

Nathan did this with David when he had to expose the Bathsheba affair. Some messages must be delivered privately. No reason exists why pastors or bishops can't be anointed in their offices just as well as in a public meeting!

Spiritual preparation before these visits to leaders is still the key, whether the prophet is male or female. The prophet must go from the prayer room to the throne room, anointed with the divine word.

Even then, rejection may still come. Male prophets are just as easily rejected as female ones. I always remind myself in those moments that they are rejecting Christ and not me. Prophets of either sex must be willing to take up their crosses and share in the fellowship of His sufferings.

The problem is larger than gender. Any prophet has trouble being heard in most of our local churches today, not just gifted women. Leaders naturally resist prophets. It is the exception rather than the rule to welcome a prophet's visitation.

Finally, God created us male and female for a purpose. I have tried to be especially sensitive to the legitimate ministries and roles God has given to males, as well as the unbiblical hang-ups about women in secular and religious cultures. This had made the work of God much easier for me.

When I come into a local church—even when it's to speak at a women's meeting—I still prayerfully visit with the pastor first, whether the person is male or female. We must give honor and respect to whom honor is due.

Bunkers of Intercession

Also, I had to learn warfare while in the trenches. The Coleman meetings were a siege at the gates of hell. We were in protracted combat, dug into our bunkers for a long spiritual battle that literally lasted years.

Our orders for battle were coming from the Holy Spirit as He gave instructions and formed us into soldiers of the next move. The Bible became our field manual, map, cookbook and guide.

Through listening prayer, our little band of intercessors held onto the altar of the Lord for one instruction after another. Like Jeremiah, we waited in the Lord's presence until *"the word of the Lord came"* to us. (This phrase appears over 50 times in the Book of Jeremiah alone!) We joined that great band of prophets that have listened for the Lord's word through the ages: Deborah, Abigail, Ezekiel, Daniel, Hosea, Joel, Amos, Jonah, Micah, Habakkuk, Zephaniah, Haggai, Zechariah, Malachi, John and the daughters of Philip.

We listened and obeyed. Our group ran with each command as it came. We were assembling as a body like a church, but the meeting was never an end in itself. We weren't really there to build a local church but to learn how to be free in the move, to unmuzzle the ox, and let the commands of God come forth.

So we began by calling the intercessors together for travail. *"As soon as Zion travailed, she gave birth to her children"* (Isaiah 66:8). We had to hear the judgment of God and grieve for the sin of our people. *"Hear the word of the Lord, O women, and let your ear receive the word of His mouth; teach your daughters wailing, and everyone her neighbor a lamentation"* (Jeremiah 9:20).

Finally, we had to take our positions as watchmen on the wall. The Lord is still looking for men and women today who *"would make up a wall, and stand in the gap before Me on behalf of the land, that I should not destroy it"* (Ezekiel 22:30).

The Coleman outpouring fell as a combination of Lent and Advent—we gathered in repentance and weeping, while waiting for the blessings of God on people and places otherwise destined for judgment.

It was a time to learn leadership skills in the prayer chamber, to speak out with authority and unction. I was horrified at times when our group seemed to go wild, boxing the air and interceding in many directions without a coordinated purpose. So I sometimes become like a drill sergeant and took charge of the prayer forces we were directing against Satan's hosts of wickedness. I learned to use Bible texts as recipes for priestly ministry, laying down rules for combat. As the Lord gave commands, I directed the flow of the meeting according to His will.

Commanding the Move

Then, I had to learn how to direct the move of God.

God spoke, *"Come up here and I will show you things to be...Now, tell Me to move."*

"Me, Lord?" I questioned. "Order You to move?"

God replied. *"Nancy, tell Me to move."*

As I gave this command in Jesus' name, the Holy Spirit of God physically rushed into Bonnie's living room "like a mighty wind." The whirlwind was real. This wasn't something limited to the spiritual world. We were all actually knocked off our feet.

There are times and situations in which a person can actually command God to move without being presumptuous. This is not trying to make God into Santa Claus. It requires that first the believer must be totally conformed to His will. God wants our agreement in order to fulfill His desires.

In Joshua 10:14, we read, *"the Lord heeded the voice of man,"* when Joshua commanded the sun and the moon to stand still. God listens and answers us when we pray for His will to be done. It's like our children asking for food; we cannot deny them. How much more will God grant us when we ask according to His will and desire? It is pleasant music to the ears of the Lord to hear us desiring what He wants.

We must not be afraid to command God to move in revival among His people and throughout the earth. He has left us here with the mission of bringing all nations to His throne. His will has been made manifest. Ask freely for righteousness, peace, justice, salvation, healing and deliverance.

God wants to give us all these things and so much more! He wants to use you to speak His will into existence. As you come across His promises in your devotional readings, you have every right to command the will of God to come to pass.

You are God's eyes and ears in your world. Christ promised that you would do even greater things than He did! He has no hands but your hands. He has no feet but your feet. When you see a situation that is absolutely wrong and outside the will of God, you don't have to sit back and do nothing. Ask yourself, "What would Christ do?" Then go ahead and do it.

Possessing the Land

Finally, the Lord Jesus Christ showed me four steps to possess the land, to bring my environment into harmony with God's will and purposes.

First, I had to **know my inheritance.** God gave us history in the Torah to show all believers in all times how to achieve God's will for their families and nations. The Bible takes great pains to define the inheritance of God's people. Moses and Joshua knew the literal boundaries of their promised land. They couldn't possess a place without a deed that defined it. God has made a similar covenant with His church today, His bride.

He has revealed His will clearly for us. As you recall in His presence what He has promised, the Lord will be *"aroused from His holy habitation"* and become *"a wall of fire around"* you (Zechariah 2:13,5). This shows why we need to measure our inheritance. When we know what is ours, we can boldly ask the Lord of Hosts to provide for us and protect His interests. *"He who touches you touches the apple of His eye"* (Zechariah 2:8).

Second, **know your enemy.** Satan is a liar and a father of lies who is out to blind our eyes to reality. (See 2 Corinthians 4:4). Things are not as they appear on TV and in the news media. They are not the way your friends say they are or the magazines at the check-out counter promise. Governments, powers and the principalities of this world do not have the final word.

The president, dictators and "the rich and beautiful" of this world don't have the final say, either. The combined firepower of all the armies, navies and air forces of this world are nothing but toy pistols to God. *"He who is in you is greater than he who is in the world"* (1 John 4:4).

Third, **tear down Satanic strongholds in your land.** Obedience is precious to God. In Deuteronomy 12:1-4, we see that before we can build a place for the Lord, we have to tear down every idol. Satan has built substitutes for God's will which he offers to the people of this world.

In prayer, we need to ask the Lord to reveal the locations and identities of these proud substitutes that have replaced Him in the hearts of the people. Then we assault them, casting down the images and gods of this age.

Fourth, **replace these idols with the worship of the Lord.** Deuteronomy 12:5-10 further explains how the strongholds of sin and disobedience must be replaced. This is the principle of binding and loosing the Lord taught in Matthew 16:19. Every unclean spirit which is cast out creates a spiritual vacuum that must be filled, or the evil spirit will return bringing others with it.

As we prayed in Coleman about this, we reread Deuteronomy and Joshua to see how God's people possessed their land. Hundreds of tips are buried in these Scriptures that will guide you in your prayers. For examples, see Deuteronomy 1:8; 11:8-24; 20:8-10; Joshua 1:8-21 and 21:43-45. By pray-reading these texts and applying them to current situations, you will be able to see the promises of God fulfilled in your life and in the lives of your loved ones.

China First and Then the World

By 1988, we knew why God has set aside those years of waiting. God had prepared us to be ready. It was time now to begin proclaiming the next move of God, an international revival that would finally present Christ our Lord with the fruits of His sacrifice. He died that all the people of this world might come to Him as His holy bride, dressed in righteousness without spot or wrinkle.

But how was I to bring these nations to Christ? Where was I supposed to begin?

A girlfriend whose husband had a ministry to Africa challenged me to join her on a mission to Nigeria. I prayed. God seemed to be giving His release. So I began to plan my first overseas mission.

Then, I met Nora Lam for the second time. Years before, this Chinese evangelist (whose life story is told in the TBN film, *China Cry*) had prophesied over me. It had been a painful and mysterious prophecy.

Now, I was invited by a friend to attend a second Love China Banquet with Nora Lam. After the banquet, she asked if I could meet alone with her the next day for breakfast.

I appeared at 6:00 AM to find Nora less glamorous but no less energetic than she had been the night before. Taking my hand in hers, Nora prophesied from the Lord, ***"You are an anointed woman of God! You must***

*come to China now! Come to China first, and then
doors will open for you around the world."*

I argued for a moment, "But I already have my
ticket for Africa!"

"China first and then the world!" she repeated
the prophesy louder and with more authority. It was the
Lord. I needed no theatrics to convince me.

I didn't even call Charles. I knew the routine by
now. I just found some table space and wrote out a faith
check for $300. On the notation line, I wrote out the
words that didn't yet express my real feelings: "Love
China!"

Chapter 12

China: When Great Walls Crumble

That I may know Him and the power of His resurrection,
and the fellowship of His sufferings,
being conformed to His death.
—Philippians 3:10

Nora Lam's predictions about my future ministry came true with amazing accuracy! By faith, I joined her on the Love China '88 mission even though my heart was set on Africa. Just as she predicted, I met people on that tour who directly led me to several other overseas missions! Through that single China mission, I went on to Nigeria, the Philippines, Russia, Thailand, the Ukraine and even back to China again! However, it was very hard to believe all that would happen when Nora Lam challenged me to drop my African trip and go to China.

Woman of Many Wounds

In 1978 the first time Nora gave a word of knowledge to me, she pointed directly at me and said mysteriously in the Spirit, *"This lady has many wounds—so many hurts and cuts."*

We had never met before then, so it was impossible for Nora to know how deeply I had suffered since entering Christ's service. All of the betrayals, rejections, failures, sleepless nights of birthing, intercessory prayer —how could she know and understand? Yet she knew the price I paid because she had paid it, too: first, in communist prison camps and later in years of coast-to-coast ministry in America.

Both of us had entered that mystical communion of sacrifice, suffering and sorrow that comes to those who take up their crosses and follow Christ in *"the fellowship of His sufferings"* (Philippians 3:10). No one who receives the ministry of intercession and prophecy can escape such pain. "No cross, no crown!" is the message of 2 Timothy 2:12; Romans 5:17; 6:5,8; 8:17; Matthew 10:33 and Numbers 23:19.

Every mother knows that without pain and bloodshed there is no birth. We give life in suffering. *"Now if we are afflicted,"* wrote Paul in 2 Corinthians 1:6, *"it is for your consolation and salvation, which is effective for enduring the same sufferings which we also suffer. Or if we are comforted, it is for your consolation and salvation."*

Paul says we are actually called to complete the sufferings of Christ. I cannot understand this, but it's an inescapable fact of life for prophets. The hardest part of the ministry has been accepting these wounds.

Woman of Many Healings

I was excited to note the change when Nora prophesied over me the second time a decade later in 1988!

"This woman has had many wounds," repeated Nora almost exactly as she had spoken before, but in the past tense, *"but she is healed now. This lady has an*

international ministry. She loves people, and the Lord will use her greatly!"

The word "international" rang in my ears like the long, vibrating echo one hears after a great bell has clapped. Nearly 18 years before, in a church basement, a friend first prophesied that I would have an "international" ministry. I had written it down then. Now it was confirmed!

Later that night, Nora called me out a second time. *"Latter rain. Latter rain,"* she said as she laid hands on me in prayer, *"I impart my anointing, everything I have into you for the end-times move."*

The Spirit revealed to me that I was being called to China before Nora said anything. Somehow, I knew that I was being invited to share her heartbeat, to love those slant-eyed, teeming millions on the other side of the Pacific Ocean.

I felt my life suddenly out of control. Nora was speaking for God, drawing me into His plans and designs. My sense of helplessness and loss of autonomy increased.

The next morning, at breakfast with Nora, I sat next to an old acquaintance, a big Afro-American woman. She also had a strong prophetic gift. The meeting was underway and so we weren't able to talk much. I didn't share my struggle with her.

By now, Nora had already called me out for China. In my heart I had decided to go, but I hadn't yet written my deposit check or told anyone of my decision. "Lord," I prayed, "Could you just give me one more sign? Some personal word to confirm that I really should go to China?"

I got up from my seat for a few minutes. When I came back, the Afro-American sister was gone. But before she left, she had scribbled out a note for me. The prophecy is so precious that I still carry it with me:

"Nancy, this is to confirm My guidance to you. I've opened doors for you to reach ambassadors and politicians of many countries. This is your initial training for the great work I've already prepared and anointed you for—training handmaidens to lead worldwide ministries, worldwide tours and foreign missions." Thus saith the Lord.

This prophecy was similar to ones repeated in Coleman year after year, but much clearer and more specific.

God has given me a "one-toot" message. My duty is to blow one note on the trumpet. Now, starting with China, I was being called to go international with the anointing.

End-times Handmaidens

The emphasis on training handmaidens was fascinating. My ministry has always attracted women to do the Lord's work in the world. God was reminding me that women are key to reaching the world for Christ.

God revealed to me some of the reasons why women are vital to His move. First, the Holy Spirit seems to touch more chords in women's hearts than in men's. Creative and responsive, we are excellent intercessors. Next, in many Muslim and Hindu countries, billions of women in harems and inner courts will never be able to hear the Gospel unless other women carry it to them. Often, women have more time and freedom to give to intercession and prophecy. Finally, women can reach ambassadors, presidents and rulers, men who often are unreachable any other way. Women can get through to these men because we are their wives and mothers.

Global Perspectives

Nora Lam was my global Lydia, not just calling me to China, but to the whole world. Suddenly, I could see the end-times international heart of God clearly!

The Lord's vision is so much larger than the USA, than our local churches, our families and our communities. Of course, we must apply our faith to local needs as well, but the eyes of Christ are on the world. We must turn our eyes where His are. He is still shedding His tears of compassion for the nations, just as He shed His blood for them on Golgotha.

Before leaving for China, I was asked to serve communion during a worship service. To my horror, I discovered that the chalice was cracked. The wine was dripping from the cup. "Oh, Jesus!" I cried under my breath, "your blood is spilling. What am I going to do?"

The Lord spoke, *"Don't worry, Nancy. I gave My blood that it should be shed, not contained. My church is too concerned about keeping My salvation in cups. I want it to spill out to the nations."*

That's why the end-times move is happening mostly overseas. God is pouring out His Holy Spirit and power where the perishing multitudes are most concentrated.

Christ for the Nations

How many of us intercede over the world map and the newspaper as Joel did over the people God gave him?

He cried out in prayer, *"Spare Your people, O Lord, and do not give Your heritage to reproach, that the nations should rule over them. Why should they say among the peoples, 'Where is their God?'"* (Joel 2:17).

In the city of Hualien, Taiwan, the Spirit led me to preach from that verse. He showed me how Chinese people are ruled and enslaved by traditions—old religions, idols, Buddhism and Marxism. In the temples of Bangkok, I saw the same bondage in action. People with blank, joyless faces bowing before speechless idols.

The nations are held in bondage by demons who tie and gag the souls of their helpless slaves. How will they ever respond to Christ and the Gospel if intercessors will not *"bind the strong man"* (Mark 3:27)? We are called to liberate a heritage for Christ in every dark corner of this globe.

China broke my heart, showing me that we need to be praying for Ankara, Canton, Kabul and Khartoum with the same fervency we pray for ourselves. Christ is standing before the Father now, ever living to make intercession for His yet unborn heritage in these forgotten cities. China permitted me to enter into the heart of Jesus in a new way as I prayed for people groups and places I hardly knew existed.

The International Language of Love

One of the most amazing discoveries I made in Hualien was the power of anointed love to overcome cultural, language and racial barriers. God uses us to pass on the anointing with a touch, a smile and a word of love—even when we're not fluent with the language. The Holy Spirit speaks all languages equally well.

Before Nora's crusades, we would fan out into the streets to distribute thousands of "Jesus Loves You" invitations. We prayed and smiled a lot, using our hands to talk. Even though I couldn't speak Chinese, our goodwill clearly got the message across. The local football stadium was packed with standing-room-only crowds.

We prayed and worshipped, breaking into circle dances and singing in English. We passed out Bibles and smiled a lot. Of course, Nora and local church leaders preached in fluent Chinese. Hundreds received salvation, deliverance and healing at the altar service.

I found Spirit-inspired love breaks through the biggest communication barriers. Since then, I have re-learned this truth repeatedly in each new country where the Lord sends our teams to minister. They know we are disciples by our love.

Bill Bray

At lunch in Canton one day, I sat across from a strange young man I had been seeing everywhere since the mission began. He was dressed in one of those bush jackets newsmen wear—the kind with 28 different pockets inside and out, front and back, up one side and down the other. He looked like Captain Kangaroo. Every one of those pockets was filled with film or notepads. He gingerly laid his twin cameras down, addressing me before he was in the chair.

Bill Bray was a missionary photojournalist. A veteran traveler, he had made dozens of overseas trips to most Asian capitals, reporting missions news. He had spent seven years in Southeast Asia during the Vietnam War.

Nora used Bill to document the mission with pictures and stories for her *China Today* newspaper. He was both reporter and editor for that publication, as well as many others.

"Do you do a newsletter?" he casually asked.

Suddenly, my heart was in my mouth. I was troubled over the failures of my first attempts at a newsletter, so he had touched a raw nerve.

We talked then about my *Trumpet's Call* newsletter ministry. I was discouraged. It took hours for me to write out the messages God had given me. Then I painfully typed and photocopied them, but it seemed to me that most folks despised these precious prophesies.

"People barely glance at my newsletters," I complained, "I never get a response to my mailings." It troubled me that I worked so hard to produce a message which I knew the Lord had given me, only to have it treated as junk mail by most of my friends.

"Well," Bill replied in a matter-of-fact tone, "that's normal. It has always been that way for prophets. Don't quit. You have to put the message in writing even when it seems that no one cares. Someone does.

"The Lord will animate and quicken the word to those for whom it is intended. The Bible promises that His Word will not return void!"

I felt my eyes snap to attention. Here was a man who believed in the written word as much as I did. He also discerned and identified my spiritual gift within seconds.

"God uses the written word in a special way," he said with increased passion. "Through the ages He has always commanded the word to be written out. I think the most important things I've ever done for God in my life have been the books I've written with other Christian leaders. Books speak on for years!"

Bill told me about the three missions bestsellers he had written with K. P. Yohannan of Gospel for Asia. He told me how the books have been used to recruit thousands of American sponsors for native missionaries.

"When I get to heaven," said Bill, "I expect to see millions who came to Christ as a result of those books. So don't give up. The best way to introduce anything new is through a book.

"The written word is always the primary medium for the prophet. That's why God chose to use a book, the Bible, to reveal His master plan for the human race."

I listened in awe, but I didn't need Bill to tell me these things. I already believed them. Underlined in my Bible were the words from Habakkuk 2:2-3, *"Write the vision and make it plain on tablets, that he may run who reads it...though it tarries, wait for it, because it will surely come."* For years I knew that I had to write.

"If you ever want help publishing your letters," Bill offered, "give me a call!" He handed me his card and rushed off with his cameras.

I tucked the card safely away in my purse. "Maybe someday," I thought, "I will call him."

Eventually, God used Bill to help me put this message in print for millions to read and to organize some of our most important overseas missions. This book was one of the results of that chance meeting in Canton!

Teresa Shaw

But Bill Bray wasn't the only miracle encounter on the Love China mission. I also met Teresa Shaw through Nora. Teresa was an evangelist's wife. We soon became friends as we ministered together.

"You know," I confided one day, "I wasn't supposed to go on this trip—I was supposed to go to Africa instead. That's where my real burden is, but God spoke through Nora, and that's why I'm here."

Teresa stopped a moment, looking at me in disbelief. "That's interesting," she said, "my husband goes to

Africa all the time. He lives for African souls!" No more was said on the China trip about Africa, but God kept bringing my words to Teresa's mind after she got home.

Unexpectedly several months later, Teresa phoned me. "I'm calling because I can't get you out of my mind," she confessed. "My husband and I are taking a team to Nigeria, and I believe that God is saying you're supposed to come to Africa with us. Are you still ready to go?"

"Ready?" I cried. "I've been ready for years. I feel God drawing me to Africa like an ant to a picnic!" I hung up, celebrating the fact that God was being true to His word. Everything was just as God promised. It was *"China first and then the world."*

Chapter 13

Africa: Mission as God's Ambassador

*You must prophesy further about many peoples,
nations, tribes, and kings.*
—*Revelation 10:11* TLB

Flanked by stone-faced staff and armed bodyguards, the General shifted curiously as I weaved toward him through a sea of shinning black faces. He sat on the dais in splendor, ruling over the gala affair. I was in Lagos, the capital of Nigeria, which is the most populous and wealthiest West African country.

My diamonds sparkled in the brilliant ballroom lights. Now I was glad I had brought my jewels for this first African preaching tour. If I listened to friends, I would have just packed tennis shoes and a bush jacket for this mission, but God had told me differently. I was not here as a tourist.

"Go as Queen Elizabeth would," said the Holy Spirit. **"I'm sending you to review My troops in Nigeria. Go in silks and pearls."**

Now I saw the reason for dressier attire. I wore silk dresses and my best jewelry nearly every day—and my hosts loved it. In fact, I didn't need sportswear even once!

This was not the storybook Africa of lions and grass huts. I was in the capital of a powerful, oil-rich military state with vast international trade.

Although I didn't fully understand it, the Lord revealed that I was *"going to powerful leaders with a powerful message."* My commission was to bring revival from the top down. So it was natural that I should start in Lagos, meeting and witnessing to the Nigerian elite.

What if I had listened to the prevailing advice of men rather than the Lord and had worn a jogging suit or missionary bush jacket? I would not have been invited into the room!

Land of Lydias and Spiritual Warfare

Africa, like a powerful magnet, attracts me year after year for crusades, missions and speaking events. The whole continent has such a hunger and openness to the Lord! Africans are eager for the move of God. They don't mind at all that an American woman brings it.

Often, just one special Lydia calls me to a place, but Africa is different. My mailbox is full of appeals and invitations from all over that huge continent. It has truly become a "land of Lydias" for our ministry.

Satan has also established great citadels of religious intolerance there, especially in the North. The gates are designed to hold the continent captive to his evil will through Islam and a host of animistic religions.

Yet this is God's hour for Africa. Church and mission growth are explosive. Many believe that Africa is replacing North America as the next Christian continent.

Africa is a place of titanic spiritual warfare. The battle between light and darkness is so intense that it often breaks into open violence. Thousands of African believers are killed every year for their faith.

Spiritual warfare is accepted as normal. Africans live with spirits and demon powers. At one church leaders' conference, there was no debate when the Lord revealed to me a Jezebel spirit of divination over Nigeria cutting off her prophets. I found instant acceptance from the pastors. They were delighted to put on the full armor of the Lord with me and command the spirit, "Come out in the Name of Jesus and free Nigeria."

The spirit of divination was broken in that room; the muzzle was taken off their mouths. *"A lion has roared! Who will not fear? The Lord has spoken! Who can but prophesy?"* Amos 3:8 was fulfilled in our midst. Several pastors rose in turn to give prophecies to their people.

The General

The General looked positively majestic in his dignified white robes. He was crowned in a gray, Persian-wool cap that was brimless in the style of the more Islamic, northern Nigerians. The heavy gold rings on both hands eloquently proclaimed that he was exactly what he looked like, a wealthy chieftain of his tribe.

Later, I learned his power in the ruling junta made him virtually the uncrowned king of Nigeria. His authority extended far beyond his tribal boundaries.

Nigeria, like so many post-colonial African states, is a federation of many tribes and territories. Besides the bigger Nigerian tribes—the Hausa, Ibo and Yoruba—there are over 426 smaller tribal groupings!

My presence at this gala concert was a miracle in itself. I really had expected to spend a quiet evening in the house. But the Lord had mapped out a different plan. He wanted me to start a spiritual relationship with the General, and He worked out the details. God always has a plan. Our job is to discover and fulfill it.

"Aren't you going to the gala concert tonight?" asked my hostess at dinner. She had a precise Oxford accent, a trademark of the private schools which graduate the ruling classes of modern Africa.

"What gala concert?" I questioned in reply, "I don't even have an invitation."

Without pausing to answer or explain, she just took charge of planning my evening. "Oh, you must go!" she said, sounding very British with mock exasperation. "Hurry! I'll have my car and driver wait for you. We'll meet you at the hotel." She ordered me to go upstairs, get dressed and be ready in 15 minutes.

From her scolding tone, it was obvious that there was nothing further to be discussed. I did as I was told, knowing God must have something very special planned.

When I returned in my blue silk dress with a simple diamond pendant and matching earrings, my hostess had already gone. But the chauffeur and car were waiting as promised.

Almost as soon as I arrived in the ballroom, I saw him. As he came into my field of view, the Lord spoke clearly to me. Although I had no idea then of the near-presidential power he wielded, I knew that I had a message from God for this modern-day king.

Like Queen Esther, I knew that somehow, someday, in some way, I would deliver the word to him. But he seemed so very, very distant and unapproachable!

"Go up and introduce yourself," urged the Holy Spirit when he got up to leave.

Gathering all my courage, I took a deep breath and walked right toward the General. I brushed past the surprised staff, ignoring protocol (and the scary-looking bodyguards) to extend my hand. Stunned at my audacity, he responded by thrusting out his hand. I felt like we were at a Kiwanis Club luncheon back home in Birmingham.

"Hi, I'm Nancy Milsk," I said with my best smile, "and I'm here from the United States at the invitation of the Bishop. Thank you for having us in your country." That was all I said. I don't even remember what pleasantry he said in reply. I didn't see him again during that first visit.

But God wasn't through with the General yet—nor with my commission to him! Even though I had no idea when, if ever, I would be back in Nigeria, the Lord had opened the door a crack for me. When He opens a door, no man can close it.

As it turned out, just five months later I was invited back to preach at the great Ibadan Convention, which was located about 45 minutes outside Lagos. I was known affectionately as "Mommy Milsk" by then.

This time, Mommy Milsk had two more divine appointments with the General! Neither was planned by man anymore than that first had been. There are no coincidences in His service, only "God-incidences!"

These meetings were the General's personal opportunities to discover incredible power from on high. As strange as it seems, God in His economy decided that He would send me all the way from Michigan to deliver the anointed word.

The first night of the convention, I sat on the dais with the other ministers. However, the second evening, there was not enough room on the platform, so I was asked to sit in a special box. Next to me was an empty chair. "I wonder who is going to sit in that seat," I asked myself, already expecting some kind of divine accident with whomever God brought to me.

I didn't have long to wait. Within minutes, the General came in, accompanied by his bodyguards. He was ushered in right next to me and seated in that empty chair. God reserved seats for us! Recognition lit up his eyes as he saw my face. But he sat with the same dignified composure as before while the Bishop began a service that lasted long into the dark night.

"Tell the General he's got to have the Holy Ghost," said a divine voice in my heart, *"but be careful how you say it!"*

Leaning over to the General, I said, "Excuse me, sir, I understand that you love the Lord."

"Oh, yes," he answered, "I do love the Lord."

Noticing that he was wearing bifocals, I reached into my purse and pulled out my own granny glasses. Slowly and dramatically, I put on my bifocals as the General watched every move with regal detachment. "Excuse me again," I asked, "but have you received the Holy Ghost since you have believed?"

"What Holy Ghost?" he asked.

Shouting to be heard over the noise of thousands praying below us, I flipped to Acts 1:2-8 where the disciples received their power. I read the story to him. "Look here," I pointed to the text, "you can't run an army without power. You don't have the power of God that He says you need!"

He stared stony-faced. Thinking that I had somehow not gotten through, I repeated emphatically, "You need the power of God!"

The audience stood for a closing hymn. Nothing more was said. Apparently happy to escape from this crazy American, the General was quickly escorted out of the room.

But God wasn't through yet! The next day, in the same convention, the General was invited to share in one of the women's meetings. I was on the program, too. The surprised General was visibly shaken to find himself seated next to me again on the speakers' platform.

The Holy Spirit spoke to me, *"Tell him again that he needs My power!"*

"Excuse me," I began, still grasping for a conversation starter, "but did you know that King David also had an army, and that he needed the power of God?"

"Where's that in the Bible?" he demanded.

"Right here in 1 Chronicles 12:32," I replied triumphantly and turned to the passage. "It says here that God gave David the wise men of Issachar as his troops. They had the Holy Spirit and were first to recognize David as the new king of Israel. David needed the power of God to recruit a special force of Spirit-filled soldiers!"

"Tell him again," said the Holy Spirit.

"You need the power of God to run your army," I said solemnly.

"Why?" asked the General, his last shed of pride striped away. It was obviously very hard for a powerful ruler like the General to accept this word from a woman —and a foreigner. Nigerians have a great sense of national pride which developed in response to British colonialism. Foreign advice is shunned. Plus, Nigerian women rarely give males any kind of advice. They are always segregated from men in public. So the Lord had to set all this up especially for both of us.

Could it be that no one on his staff or in his entire family could get through with this word? Probably the only way God could speak to him was to send a white woman from Detroit!

I thought of another general, Naaman the leper, who also had to humble himself and receive the gift of healing on the Lord's terms rather than his own. But the that day, the General did. He left the hall a new man with the power of God burning afresh in his heart.

In his testimony later, the General looked at me and especially commented on how wonderful it was that we could all be together in unity—men and women, African and Anglo. Yet, when the prayers ended and it came time to say good-bye, an awkward silence reminded us both of the cultural barriers that still separated an American lady preacher from an African general.

I could see that he wanted to give me a big hug but the man-made walls of tradition, sex and race stood between us. We both felt the love, born of God, that makes us one in Christ, and love won out. With a shrug that seemed to say what words could not, he ignored his aides and the bystanders. I disappeared into a huge bear hug of thanks.

Team Ministry

In Nigeria, the Lord knit me together with Jacque Heasley in a unique team ministry. We have since traveled together on a number of missions to Africa and other countries. I'd never met anyone who worked so well with me in the Spirit, not just on the platform, but before and after the ministry in our prayer chambers.

Jacque was very good at birthing and travailing, helping to bring in the revival move. Before meetings she prepared the way in our hearts first, binding us together as one. Then in the meetings, she had a wonderful gift of music and worship that led the people to the very door of the tabernacle. By the time I brought forth the word, her ministry already had established the whole room in oneness and unity with God.

Right on the spot, Jacque often knew just what to do in order to take us into the heavenlies. She also had the boldness to take authority and act.

In one crusade on the Athi River near Nairobi, Kenya, we were brought up to minister before the people had entered into worship. At first, the crowd was cold and unresponsive to the praise which Jacque began to lead. The move of God had not started. Spontaneously, Jacque pulled me up on my feet, took my hand and said, "Come on Nancy, let's worship, even if no one else will!"

Without any explanation, we entered immediately into the Holy of Holies together. Our unity attracted the Holy Spirit. In a heartbeat the crusade was transformed. We melted into one with the people. When we dropped to our knees on the rough boards of the platform, the entire audience followed without commands or directions.

Soon the Spirit anointed me and my interpreter. I was led to act out and preach about Mary at the garden tomb. Listeners were transfixed by the power of God. The native interpreter and I were so submitted to God that we spoke as if we had one voice.

Even today I receive letters about what happened next. Many of those who were there have since taken that anointing back to their villages. Still they are asking us to return and lead more people into the power of God.

An Anointing Wave

Foreign languages and overseas travel in strange cultures has made it easier for me to stay humble and let the Holy Spirit flow in fresh ways. Since any communication skills I have in English are gone, I am thrown upon the Lord in childlike dependence. This is great training for anyone bringing in new moves of God because of the constant reminder that revival comes *"not by might, nor by power, but by my Spirit, says the Lord of hosts"* (Zechariah 4:6).

The Lord taught me this when I was invited to speak in what was then a small mission church. Publicity for Mommy Milsk had been great. Several hundred came to the opening service. The preliminaries seemed to go on forever. There was an hour of deadly announcements.

I was eager to speak. My message was all set. In fact, I was getting impatient. Finally, after a big build up from the organizer, I was in the pulpit.

As I opened my mouth, the Lord just told me to wait awhile and say nothing—I mean nothing at all! Needless to say, this got everyone's attention. I felt my cheeks redden in embarrassment.

Then I felt some liberty to start speaking on my chosen subject, "The Shekinah Glory Cloud." For some reason the interpreter could not understand me or the subject. A tense, embarrassed hush came over the hall.

God spoke in that teasing inner-city Detroit sarcasm He uses whenever He wants to teach me a personal lesson, *"Well, Nancy, what are you going to do now? Don't you think it's time to rely on Me?"*

I was ready. The Lord didn't have to ask twice.

God instructed me, *"Ask the interpreter for the word 'holy'."*

"Mema," said the interpreter.

"Now ask the interpreter for the word 'glory'."

"Ogoo," came the reply.

"Now," said God to make sure I got the point, *"You get out of the pulpit and start saying 'mema, mema, mema, ogoo, ogoo, ogoo.'"*

I felt utterly foolish. It sounded like baby talk to me. However, I obeyed the Lord and started to worship Him, saying, "Mema, mema, mema, ogoo, ogoo, ogoo."

Looking up, I saw the glory cloud above the people. Hundreds rose to their feet, breaking into ecstatic adoration. All barriers were broken down between the many denominations, languages and tribes in the room. Hundreds chanted in one voice of praise "Mema! Mema! Mema! Ogoo! Ogoo! Ogoo!" It was majestic and awesome.

Learning Obedience in Public

The Lord constantly repeats this lesson. The day before I ministered at one big convention, an African woman prophesied that God would move greatly—only if I would obey exactly.

The next day, the Lord spoke to me during the invitation of another speaker during the women's meeting. It really wasn't my turn to speak, and the invitation was almost over. *"Nancy, I want these women to have the fullness of My Spirit, the tenth portion, the Benjamin portion."*

I argued a little with God, "Lord, there's no time to explain all that to the people. Ten women have already come to receive the baptism of the Holy Spirit, and five are going back to their seats!"

"Remember the five wise virgins who filled their vessels and were ready for the bridegroom? Fill the vessels of these women who are here today.

"Go to the microphone. Blow into it and count to ten."

Now I really felt stupid. "Lord, this is not my platform. I'm out of order. People will think I'm foolish!" But then I remembered the woman who said God would move greatly only if I obeyed. God sometimes has a different order than man's.

"Okay, Lord," I said, "I'm obeying You exactly!"

I went to the mike and blew into it. People looked at me strangely. I counted to ten: "One...two...three...four ...five...six...seven...eight...nine...ten!" Then I saw it as promised. The Shekinah-glory cloud again appeared, hovering over the women. He was going to fill their vessels to overflowing!

Suddenly, the power of God swept across the room. Hundreds collapsed into their chairs, many falling to the floor under the power of God's awesome presence. A Holy Spirit wave literally knocked the people off their feet.

His ways are not our ways. He delights in breaking our traditions and demonstrating His power differently. We cannot comprehend or control Him! News of that outpouring spread quickly to the rest of the convention.

Years later, people are still talking about it. It started a sustained revival which has made that church one of the biggest missionary outreaches in all Nigeria.

The Roar of God

Standing in the wings at the great Redemption Camp Meeting near Lagos, the Bishop turned and spoke, "Now, Nancy, I want you to be sure to hear something and remember it as you fly back home.

"Amos says, *'The Lord roars from Zion,'* and that's what you're about to hear, the Lord roaring from His African Zion!"

As we stepped onto the platform, a low rumbling began to swell up from the 20,000 voices that stretched out before us. Within seconds the roar became strong enough to drown out even the loudest Super Bowl crowd. It turned into songs of praise. Sound waves from human voices literally shook the platform and filled the air with an invisible force.

Before me I saw an ocean of different people—folks from various traditions, denominations, classes, cultures, tribes and genders. All praised the Lord together in their own languages—Hausa, Ibo, Yoruba and so many others. (Over 510 languages are spoken in the Nigerian churches!)

The unified roar still rang in my ears as my plane landed in the States.

Why Not Here At Home?

Walking the sterile halls of Kennedy International Airport, a cry rose from my heart, "Why, Lord? Why is your move so strong in Nigeria and so weak here in the United States?"

In Africa, the five-fold ministry routinely operates in meetings. The Lord's anointed come together in unity. Where unity is, the blessing of God flows down, *"like the precious oil...on the beard of Aaron"* (Psalm 133:2).

No wonder Paul says the greatest charismatic gift is love. That is the secret to both power and unity. Prayer, fasting and repentance are important, but love more so!

I have no formula for revival, but I think that one big reason Africans are receiving more from God right now is their willingness to practice greater love for one another. Many Africans demonstrate a tender love that seeks unity above self. They network with each other, submitting their ministries to the leadership of the Holy Spirit and to each other.

Our American culture trains us to put self first. We make the mistake of thinking our programs must be bigger and stronger than others in order to see revival! We insist the revival move must come through our personal ministry, church or denomination, or we don't want it.

Well, God doesn't work that way. You can't organize the move of God or bring in revival like a political campaign. I'm crazy enough to believe that the next revival move of God in the United States will begin as we simply love one another. It will start as we yield to each other, humbly letting the Holy Spirit move through other ministries, as well as our own.

Chapter 14

Moscow: Nothing Is Impossible with God

Is anything too hard for the Lord?
—Genesis 18:14

I can do all things through Christ who strengthens me.
—Philippians 4:13

My heart raced as I punched out the 214 area code on my phone pad. I prayed, waiting for a connection to North Dallas. The phone seemed to ring forever.

Would Bill Bray even remember me? It had been three years since we last talked in Canton, China about *The Trumpet's Call* newsletter. But God kept his name alive in my heart.

Someone finally answered the phone. A loud, male voice spoke. His hurried, three word greeting came out sounding like one word, "BILLBRAYHERE!" It was as if he were still answering the city desk phone in a newsroom somewhere. In the background, I could hear the noisy clacking of a teleprinter, just like in an old-fashioned newspaper office.

"You probably don't remember me," I apologized, "but I'm Nancy Milsk from Detroit. We met in China."

A nervous laugh came across the line. "Oh, yes, I do. I remember you! You won't believe this but my wife and I just prayed for you this morning. I've got your Trumpet Ministries card right here. I'm looking at it now!" He explained that while Ivy was praying with him for new assignments that morning, he had just come across my long-forgotten calling card.

I Find My Baruch

"Well," I said, "God is answering both our prayers. I'm calling to ask you to be my Baruch. I need someone to help me with my newsletters and book."

"Baruch?" asked Bill.

"Yes," I said, "don't you remember how Jeremiah worked with Baruch, the scribe?"

"I'm not sure," Bill answered. A bit of his native, inner-city Chicago sarcasm came through. "Isn't that the guy who had to run and hide for his life when the cops went after Jeremiah?"

"That's right," I said, cracking a smile in my voice. "Without Baruch's help, Jeremiah could never have sent his prophetic letters and books to King Jehoiakim. Baruch was his editor and co-author!

"I need you to polish my message so it can be published and not burned in the fires of rejection. I want to make sure the Johoiakims of this world can't stop it. Will you help me?"

There was a pregnant silence on the other end as Bill struggled for words. "Can you afford this call?" he asked. "You know we ask our ministry clients to share in our expenses, to pay by the hour. It's the only way we can operate this ministry."

I winced at the talk of finances. But I knew that I had to just close my eyes and invest. Getting out God's word was my mission in life. I had to pay the price. "God told me to call you!" I replied, "and I need a Baruch now."

In March, 1984—long before I met Bill—the Lord had applied to my life and ministry the same command to record His words that He had given Jeremiah. I underlined and dated the verse in my Bible:

> *Thus speaks the Lord God of Israel, saying: "Write in a book for yourself all the words that I have spoken to you."* *(Jeremiah 30:2)*

Only later, in chapter 36, did I find how Jeremiah did this. He actually dictated the words as they were revealed. Then Baruch, a professional writer on the temple staff, edited it.

Finally Bill spoke, "Nancy, I think you're an answer to our prayers. I'll be your Baruch. I can start your newsletter now, but I can't do the book until we get back from overseas. We're leading a mission team to Russia."

There Are No Closed Countries

"Russia?" I asked in awed reverence. My heart almost stopped beating at the sound of the word. "How can you do that? God called me to go to Russia long ago, but the Communists won't let anyone in, will they? Russia is a closed country."

"There are no closed countries anymore," said Bill matter-of-factly. "There's always a way in to any mission field. Officially, we're going as tourists, but we're taking Bibles with us just like we did in China."

Images flashed across my mind of student prayer meetings in Mount Pleasant when God called me to go to

Russia. I said "yes" then, never believing a way would be opened. Now my new Baruch was going. I had a door!

My heart was in my throat. Would he think I was crazy if I told him I wanted to go?

I wondered if Bill were planning intercession on the mission. He didn't mention it. Did he have the know-how to attack spiritual strongholds? Did he have a prophet on his team? Did he even know he needed one?

God interrupted, *"This is it. You promised Me you would go to Russia. Tell Bill you're going with his team. Tell him now."*

"Bill," I said, "I must go with you. You need a prayer leader for this mission. I usually pray about these things and talk to my husband first, but the Holy Spirit just told me that I was to join you on the Russian mission."

"Me, too," said Bill in soft wonder. "Send me your deposit, and I'll call the travel agency today. I don't know why, but I'm sure God wants you on this team even though I hardly know you."

It was that divine rush again. There was no need to intercede about it because I already had prayed. A Holy Spirit train was pulling out of the station. I was not going to be left on the platform!

I was absolutely sure, so I hung up, sat down and wrote out a $200 faith check. My decision was tested immediately. Like any other bold attack against Satan's kingdom, it brought a savage counter-attack from hell.

The Winds of Testing

Doubts hit me with gale force that night. Had I made a fool of myself? Lying demons were sent against my mind to suggest worry and fear. Within days, both my daughter Lynn and my elderly mother experienced terrible attacks from Satan.

"How can you think about going overseas now?" accused a legion of demons. "What if your mother has a heart attack in the night and dies when you aren't there for her? What about your daughter and granddaughter? You can't leave them with Charles. What kind of mother are you, anyway?"

I fretted for several nights. In the daytime hours, I called Bill and Ivy in Texas and asked them to pray with me. I reasoned and rationalized with myself, debating the wisdom and logic of this trip. The more I tried to reason with Satan, the stronger the attacks became!

My daughter Lynn had relapses. My mom called even more frequently at all hours day and night. She seemed to be getting more fanciful and forgetful. I was scared by her rapid deterioration. We got a practical nurse to come stay with her for awhile, but that didn't work out.

Finally, it came to a head. One restless night I got up at 3:00 AM and prayed in growing terror. I felt the oppression of the enemy bearing down on the whole house. This was a panic attack like none I'd ever had before. I felt as if the legions of hell were all ganging up on me, screaming at me.

My faith failed. Desperately, like a drowning victim going down for the third time, I cried out to Jesus for help. He took my hand. Suddenly, I realized that He had been there all the time. Why hadn't I called on His name earlier?

Christ spoke, *"Nancy, if you follow Me in this move, I'll take care of your family."*

"Yes, Lord" I gasped. "Forgive me for doubting. I'll follow you all the way to Siberia if you want."

It was still winter, but I felt the Lord drawing me to open a window anyway. The cold slapped my face. The sky was starless and pitch black. Recalling my special family promise verses from Isaiah 54, I leaned out and peered into the darkness.

"Satan and all you demons!" I whispered into the night, "take your hands off my family. Get away from this house and out of my life. I'm going to Russia on a mission for Christ, and you can't stop me!"

Then I quietly repeated the verses from memory, personalizing God's promises to me: *"All [my] children shall be taught by the Lord, and great shall be the peace of [my] children ...No weapon formed against [me] shall prosper!"* (Isaiah 54:13,17). The storm of doubt was over as quickly as it had begun.

I sat down and wrote a check for the rest of my Mission to Moscow contribution. I was committed now. There was no turning back. I walked to the mailbox and dropped it in with a prayer. I was obeying the Lord and going to Russia by faith.

Satan backed off right away. Everything went fine from then on. In fact, my mom didn't leave this world for another five years, and she had no problems during the whole trip. Lynn and my family managed wonderfully, too!

What happened to me is a pattern almost every Christian leader can testify about. When you obey the Lord in some really important matter, Satan will rush you with every dirty trick in the book. Often the attack is not purely spiritual. Demons will use the cares of the world—business, career, family or finances—to throw you off the right track. He'll manipulate other weak believers and leaders to instill fear.

These attacks come in a thousand ways, but they are as certain as labor pains in pregnancy. For some reason, God allows them. He does not send them, but He does not stop them. They are part of preparation for service.

Remember, God has given us spiritual weapons to resist such attacks and defeat the enemy. He sends special graces and strength as you pray. We really can *"do all things through Christ who strengthens [us]"* (Philippians 4:13).

The Amazing Power of Unity

On the Mission to Moscow outreach, the Lord put together witnessing teams of total strangers who chose to unite quickly under the Holy Spirit. What a difference it made. As a result, the Lord accomplished miracles that would have taken months and years of normal ministry.

Bill Bray's mission team to Russia was an amazing mix of people, a wild variety of religious zealots from just about every religious tradition. But they were supremely motivated by love rather than doctrine, by service to Christ in mutual submission. There were no plans to build a particular church, denomination or movement.

God selected the team. He brought those who should have been with us, and He kept those at home that were not His choices. The "chemistry" was right. The sense of worshipful expectancy was almost tangible. A prayerfulness and watchfulness came upon us as a gift from above. But I still wondered how Bill was ever going to get these people to work together.

In our first meeting, Bill called everyone together and reminded us why we were on the mission in the first place. "Many of you are meeting each other for the first time today," he said. "We come from different parts of the country. We are of different races, cultures and classes. We have different church traditions. Humanly speaking, we're sitting on a keg of dynamite. If any of us begin to minister in the flesh, this mission will blow up in our faces. So let's just be the body of Christ, mobilized to do His will in the power of the Holy Spirit."

Miraculously, the miracle of this humble call for unity held throughout the trip. There were occasions when side issues started to flare up, but almost everyone had the grace from God to spot these quickly and repent of sin immediately.

God gave us the grace to love one another and esteem each other better than ourselves. As a result, the joy of the group was a spiritual magnet to the depressed, grim Russians we met. Our presence brought Christ wherever we went. People stopped on the street to stare at us in curious wonder. We were attractive for God. Team members literally glowed with the Holy Spirit.

We were drunk with the Spirit of the Lord and publicly prayed before meals in an officially atheistic state. Songs of praise spontaneously broke out on buses and whenever the group gathered. We were a movable spiritual feast.

The Russians simply didn't know how to handle us. Most had never seen God manifested before in a group.

Word spread quickly that we had Bibles in our luggage. Almost daily, Russians came up secretly to ask for Bibles and to inquire about our faith. Many kissed and fondled the forbidden book when they received it.

Starved for Salvation

Often, Russians were so hungry for salvation that they accepted the Gospel after only minutes of explanation. At a famous cathedral in what was then downtown Leningrad, a high school student approached Bill. She asked if she could practice her English.

Bill agreed. The cathedral had been turned into a museum, so they talked about the art. "What do you think of our paintings?" she asked, pointing to the beautiful frescos. "They tell the whole Bible story in pictures."

"These are not just the story of the Bible," Bill told her. "These pictures depict the story of salvation, how God has reached down to us in love from the beginning in Genesis to the end in Revelation. Do you believe that God loves you and sent Christ to save you?" he asked.

"I want to believe," came the reply, with tears in her eyes. She was ready for conversion. Right then and there Bill prayed with her to accept Christ as Savior. In less than fifteen minutes, a new life came to Christ.

Miracle salvation appointments like this occurred daily. Everywhere police and authorities seemed powerless to keep us from witnessing. The glasnost policy of Gorbachev included freedom to discuss religion, even though anti-missionary laws were still on the books.

In Moscow's famous First Baptist Church, we visited while Chuck Colson was preaching. When he gave an invitation, a teenage girl came forward to accept Christ. "She's not 18!" exclaimed one person, pushing the girl back from the altar. "It's illegal for her to convert."

"Let her come to Christ," said another. Soon a scuffle began as one parishioner tried to push her forward and another tried to push her back! The service halted as the debate raged.

Finally, the girl stayed put and prayed to receive Christ—an unthinkable crime only weeks before. It was still completely illegal on the books.

Both of our university-trained tourist guides were so impressed that they accepted Christ in tears after hearing the Gospel! One communist guide was so radically transformed that she brought her young husband to meet us. He spent the next 24 hours reading the New Testament we gave him.

She also announced that she was pregnant and would have her baby rather than the abortion demanded by government rules. We held a spontaneous baby shower on the bus, collecting a special offering. Such an outpouring of grace was too much. Russians normally hate to receive anything without giving something back. She broke down sobbing, unable to comprehend the love of God being demonstrated by her new Christian family.

All around we saw spiritual life being born in a land where Christians had been imprisoned, murdered and persecuted for over 70 years.

Conquering the Land

Each morning, we began by gathering in small groups before breakfast. These hotel-room prayer and praise meetings were the secret of our power. We were able to break up the fallow ground and tear down strongholds that had so long controlled this land. The morning meetings made the day's harvest ready.

We prayed toward all points on the compass. Turning north, south, east, and west in turn, we would claim Deuteronomy 11:24-25, *"Every place on which the sole of your foot treads shall be yours...No man shall be able to stand against you: The Lord your God will put the dread of you and the fear of you upon all the land where you tread."*

Going over the day's itinerary, we would name the places where we were going, using prophetic prayer to bind and loosen Satan's power and control over each site. During the day we continued to pray-walk our way through the itinerary. We would claim God's authority over idols the Communists had erected as emblems of their control.

In Red Square, I became a tourist and started to stand in line at Lenin's Tomb to view the corpse of Communism's dead architect. God spoke, *"Why do you want to see Lenin's dead body? Instead, bind the spirit of death in this place. Loose the spirit of life, and plead My blood over Red Square."*

Later that year, I watched the May Day celebrations in Red Square on CNN-TV as then President Gorbachev was booed off the platform. Prophetic prayers were answered! Red Square was no longer a place of communist power and pride, but a place of Communism's defeat.

In what was still Leningrad, we pray-walked seven times around the perimeter of the model city at the WWII memorial. We claimed it for God, loosing it from communist control. Less than two years later, I heard the announcement that the city fathers had voted to change the name back to St. Petersburg, it's original Christian name!

In Kiev our bus stopped before a huge statue of Mother Russia. As dramatic as the Statue of Liberty in New York Harbor, this huge monstrosity overlooked the strategic defenses of the city. It symbolized the fact that the Ukraine was a subservient pawn, expendable in the defense of Russia.

We realized the enormous spiritual significance of the idol. That night we went into a season of intensive, travailing prayer to cast down the demon which ruled from that image. In this way we spiritually loosened the grip of communist control over the Ukraine. Within a year, the Ukraine declared independence from Russia.

Again, prophetic prayers were answered. God called us as foreign prophets to witness and to give birth to spiritual life during an amazing moment in that nation's history!

God revealed to us what He was going to do again and again, as we cast down powers and principalities. He was praying through us with images and visions of future events no one dared speak openly about at the time.

Remember, no one knew then which way the USSR would go. Many believed, with good reason, that the Communists would end glasnost and perestroika, plunging the land back into another generation of terror, torture and spiritual slavery. Humanly speaking, it could have gone either way. But God had said "enough" and revealed His plans for the destruction of the USSR to us.

Our prayer team was basically a group of housewives, untrained in geo-politics. Yet God saw fit to share His supernatural insight with us about historic and political situations we barely understood. God never overthrows nations and cultures without revealing His plans to His prophets.

Dressing in Spiritual Armor

In morning prayer and praise, one of the team always led us in a second spiritual exercise, dressing for warfare. We didn't leave our hotel unless we were certain that all six weapons of combat were inspected, cleaned and in good working order, and that we were *"praying always with all prayer and supplication in the Spirit"* (Ephesians 6:18).

If any piece of our combat gear is not in place, the powers of darkness have a weak point they can exploit. These weapons apply in every life circumstance—school, work or home.

First, truth protects our stomachs and thighs. A blow to the groin or stomach can cripple a person long enough for Satan to do even greater damage. Everything starts with truth. We have to realistically evaluate our situation, never lying to ourselves or others.

Second, righteousness protects our hearts and lungs. A Christian living in any unconfessed sin or practicing injustice is making a fatal mistake. Ultimately, the God who is always holy and perfect cannot defend us while we are in sin although He is merciful and full of grace.

Third, peace protects the soles of our feet. Empire builders are always asking for trouble. Christians are not to go out seeking a fight, but, as peacemakers, proclaiming God's love and desire to reconcile all people to Himself.

Fourth, faith shields us all over. When the flaming missiles of Satan's hatred are launched against us, we lift up faith against them. Faith is versatile and portable, able to be moved to wherever protection is needed.

Fifth, salvation covers our brains. The mind is Satan's favorite area of attack. He enjoys toying with our emotions, imaginations and perceptions. His efforts to manipulate these are futile when we plead the shed blood against them. Christ has saved us from his wiles through the cross.

Sixth, the word of God ends the attack. Ultimately, the enemy runs from our only offensive weapon, the promises of God. The covenants we have made with God will ultimately destroy Lucifer and bring death to all enemies of Christ. Knowing the will of God and declaring it to Satan defeats him every time.

It is interesting to me that Paul warns us to use the *"whole armor of God"* (Ephesians 6:11) in our spiritual warfare. No one of these weapons is effective if used alone. Overdependence on one leaves us vulnerable elsewhere.

Is Anything Too Hard for the Lord?

In Leningrad, the Lord gave me a word of revelation to help our intercession team pray to the heart of the matter: *"Nancy, the blood of Cain and Abel has been shed over this land. Release the blood of the Lamb to cleanse, liberate and sanctify this land for Me."*

There is an awesome difference between doing evangelism or intercession in the power of the flesh and doing it in the power of the Spirit. We found the people of the USSR to be bound by many evil spirits, but longing to be free. Yet, only spiritual warfare sets the captive free. That was the secret of our whole Mission to Moscow.

One morning, the rest went out for ministry, but a few stayed behind to pray in the breakfast room. It was an empty lounge with a piano, so we found it a perfect place for praise. We never asked for permission. We just spontaneously began to go into intercession and worship.

In our spirits, the Lord showed us that much blood has been shed over the land and murdering spirits had been loosed on the Russian people. But we saw the Lord wanted to change all that and have His blood flow in to bring new life to the land. There is life in the shed blood of Jesus, but death in the blood shed by men—the blood shed by Cain.

As we interceded, someone went to the piano and began singing songs of praise. Taking our eyes off man, we went to worship Him. Only then did the word of the Lord come to me: *"Nancy, now release the blood of the Lamb!"*

As we did, the Russian hotel staff began visiting the room one by one, asking us for Bibles. As they left with their Bibles, they told others. Soon all kinds of people were coming in: bellboys, busboys, doormen, kitchen staff, maids, management staff, policemen, prostitutes, taxi drivers—virtually the whole hotel! We took turns going to our rooms for more Bibles as praise continued. About 300 people were drawn to us without advertising, permissions, promotion, or planning!

Many stopped to listen to the songs even though they often couldn't understand all the words. Yet the presence and love of God was coming through. Some cried. Some hugged us. Many were saved, and others just wanted us to pray for them.

The anointing breaks yokes of bondage. It unshackles and sets the prisoners free. Praise and worship broke barriers of culture, fear, politics, religion, tradition and unbelief.

A video news crew from the local TV station appeared to capture the excitement of all these happy foreign visitors singing and enjoying their hotel. It was incredible to see the children of this world attracted to the move of God—even when they didn't really understand it.

It was that way with the Jesus movement in the 1960s and the born-again movement in the 1970s. It will be that way again when the next move of God sweeps through your life and community. The Lord is swiftly moving in these last days and is waiting to move again in your community.

This kind of miracle move isn't just something you read about in history books. It's not just for overseas, for Russia and the Ukraine, for third-world missions in Africa, Asia and Latin America. The next move of God is for you. It's for today.

The Lord Jesus Christ is calling out an army now who will do two things: first, enter into His Holy of Holies and search the Scriptures to receive God's vision for their worlds; and, second, move in faith and obedience to possess it.

Have you considered entering into the anointing that I've been describing here? Have you considered becoming an agent for Christ in your community? God wants us to have this kind of powerful ministry far more than we are seeking it! He is not denying you or your church this blessing.

Up to this point, this whole book has been a prelude. In the next chapter, I will show you how you can have the Caleb anointing operating in your life, the power of God to possess your land for Christ Jesus.

Chapter 15

The Caleb Anointing: Empowered by God

But My servant Caleb, because he has a different spirit in him and has followed Me fully, I will bring into the land where he went, and his descendants shall inherit it.
—Numbers 14:24

Are you intrigued by what you've read in these pages? Do you desire to be empowered by God, to reach your world as I have mine—to "possess the land" He has promised personally to you?

Are you wondering if the kind of life and ministry I've been writing about could be for you, too? The answer is a resounding "Yes!" The lifestyle and power I've been describing here is God's plan for **every** believer, not just for a spiritual elite, the educated or the ordained. It is not limited to the beautiful, the gifted, the rich or the talented.

If you have come to the conclusion that somehow the prophetic lifestyle I live is unobtainable, then this book has been be a massive failure. Please see me for what I am: an ordinary housewife who has been extraordinarily used of God. He didn't make an exception in my case.

Most of all, I want you to know that the power to live as I do is for you, too! Within Christ's work on Calvary is the provision for everything you will ever need to possess your personal "promised land."

If this is so—and my life is living proof that is—then why do so many Christians live with so much less than God intended?

How We Discovered the Caleb Anointing

In the darkest winter days of 1990, God showed our tiny team of Coleman intercessors that no believer need live in defeat or failure. We only pass through wildernesses times; we don't die in them as unbelievers do! Caleb's "cross-over-into-Jordan" spirit is still available to each of us today!

To learn about it, God brought me back into a wilderness time of my own. I had completed successful missions to Africa, China and Russia, but then the ministry stalled again. Nothing was happening. I felt like I was at a dead end. So I retreated to wait upon the Lord with Mel and Bonnie.

As we prayed, Arctic winds whipped against the house, drifting snow against the front porch in large swirls. The blizzard soon imprisoned us. We were surrounded by deserts of windswept snow, cut off from the outside world by the howling winds. The elements added to my spiritual gloom.

After an unusually quiet supper, we began travailing. In slacks, Bonnie and I easily fell to the living room floor in order to seek a fresh visitation of the Holy Spirit. Mel joined us, and revelation began as we prayed that God would give us something fresh from His written word.

Pray-reading Hebrews 12:18-24, we entered into the general assembly of the firstborn, mingling our praises with those mighty heroes, seeking guidance from the Lord Jesus. "How can we receive the promises and possess our land as they did?" I cried aloud in despair. My spirit marveled at the tenacity of these *"spirits of just men made perfect"* (v. 23).

Hundreds of fulfilled promises and answered prayers were forgotten as I wept before God. At that moment only the unfulfilled promises seemed to stare back at me! "What are we missing?" I begged. "Give us specific instructions, Lord! We want to march forward to possess the land!"

I turned instinctively to the Book of Numbers, reviewing again the well-worn passages I almost knew by heart. "What have I missed?" I asked, reviewing the familiar story of Caleb and Joshua.

Caleb's Obedient Faith

That's when the Lord opened our eyes to see the spirit of Caleb, a spirit of obedience that caused him to believe while millions scoffed around him. He boldly disagreed with the majority report!

Prophecy gushed from my mouth as Bonnie and Mel joined in affirmation. We needed that spirit, the same *"spirit of just men made perfect."* We laid hands on one another, asking for an outpouring of Caleb's anointing on our lives. That night all three of us were freshly empowered, professing incredible faith. Once again we were binding and loosing in prophetic prayer.

It didn't stop there. The next day we called others to join us. They too asked to receive this fresh outpouring.

I wrote a testimony of what had happened and sent it to a pastor in Texas. He called back and asked if I would come to share this message with his congregation. "This is just what I've been looking for!" he exclaimed. That Sunday night, the pastor and his entire elder board came forward to receive the Caleb anointing.

We published the Caleb anointing teaching in the *Trumpet's Call* newsletter and Bill Bray's newspaper under the banner headline, "You Need a Caleb Anointing!"

Since then, the message has swept around the world. Overseas leaders are inviting me to come, saying the Caleb-anointing message is changing their churches, their missions and their personal lives.

God Rewards Obedient Faith

Numbers 13 and 14 tell the actual Caleb story. Sent with twelve spies to survey the land promised to Israel, Caleb came back with a positive report. *"Let us go up at once and take possession,"* he urged, *"for we are well able to overcome it"* (v. 13:30).

Caleb and Joshua knew that anything God promised was theirs to possess. They simply took God at His word! However, the ten others focused on circumstances, destroying the faith of the people with negative reports on enemy strength.

As a result, only Joshua and Caleb were rewarded with life in Canaan. They choose to exercise obedient faith in the face of powerful opposition.

We need to see that we face the same choices today. The nations are our inheritance. The whole earth is our promised land. Will we believe the promise of the Lord and possess our rightful inheritance? Or will we back down, allowing fear of today's giants to discourage us?

Now is the time for us to go to the bank and cash in our spiritual winnings. All the nations and peoples of the earth have been promised to Christ. It is our task to prepare the bride of Christ for her wedding day by bringing the gentile nations to their Savior.

Moving Your Spiritual Mountain

Christ promised us mountain-moving power to overcome the enemy. How many of your personal mountains have you identified and removed yet? Does your heart ache today to see His glory manifested in some unresolved battleground of your personal world—in your marriage, in the lives of your children, in your church, family, school or community? Are there people in your life without Christ or in bondage to addictions and sin? Are there neighborhoods, streets, or places in your community without a living witness for Christ?

What do you want to see done about the spiritual mountains in your city, state or national government? The big problems of corruption, injustice and prejudice? What about current moral issues such as abortion, anti-family legislation, crime and immorality?

Then, are you bothered about the condition of your business, career, finances or health?

Finally, and most importantly, what do you desire for the lost millions still without Christ or a gospel witness? Does your heart burn to reach the unreached across town and across the sea?

If these kinds of burdens concern you, then your calling is the same as ours. You desperately need the spirit of Caleb to exercise God's rule over these areas.

Is the Caleb Anointing for Everyone?

Being used to usher in God's move is a privilege available to every willing Christian. This mantle is for any Elisha who is willing to ask and wait for it to fall from heaven. We serve the God of *"whosoever believes..."*

Caleb was not the only one called to the promised land. It was the rightful inheritance of millions! Nor was Caleb the only one given opportunity to believe. All Israel had witnessed the Lord's miraculous deliverance from Egypt with signs and wonders. They were all daily eyewitnesses to His spiritual glory at the tabernacle and physical provision through manna!

But when the test of faith came, only Caleb the prophet and Joshua the commander said "yes" to God. They entered Canaan, leading the orphaned children of those who refused to believe. The rest of the adults wandered for forty wasted years, their corpses left to rot on the wrong side of the Jordan. What a tragic choice they made, and what a tragic choice any Christian makes today who follows them in faithless disobedience.

How to Receive the Caleb Anointing

The story of Moses and the millions who died in the wilderness is one of the saddest in the Bible. It is given as a warning to God's people in all ages, a reminder that we need to cultivate the spirit of Caleb. Without it we are as doomed as the Jews who fell in Sinai.

How can we avoid their sin and have the spirit of Caleb? The Lord showed us three keys to receiving the Caleb anointing.

First, you receive the Caleb anointing by faith. The Bible says Caleb had *"another spirit"* that was entirely different from the fear, greed and disobedience that motivated the rest of Israel. The basic difference was that Caleb's spirit willfully applied his faith. The others choose to apply their spirits of unbelief.

Christians should find it easy to accept the spirit of Caleb since we have already received salvation, the Holy Spirit and our sanctification by faith. Faith is the first key. *"Without faith it is impossible to please Him"* (Hebrews 11:6). You cannot have the spirit of Caleb without having a spirit of belief.

As you review the list of faith heroes in Hebrews 11, it is amazing to see that all died with an active, obedient faith—even though many never lived to see the object of their faith and hope come to pass!

How much easier it should be for us, Christ's bride, to exercise obedient faith. We already have the down payment on our salvation in the indwelling Holy Spirit.

Second, we must enter into the fellowship of *"just men made perfect."* This is the next key to understanding the Caleb anointing. It actually defines what the spirit of Caleb is. Who are these *"just men"*? Where are they now? What characterizes their lifestyles and testimonies?

The answer is revealed in Hebrews 12, particularly verses 22-24. We find the *"spirits of just men"* are now located in the city of the living God, heavenly Jerusalem! All the Calebs of ages past are gathered there now, and they surround us like a cloud of heavenly witnesses. These are the Old Testament saints. We are being scheduled to join them in eternity as soon as we finish running our race of faith!

Chapter 12 is one long invitation to join these heroes in the general assembly and church of the firstborn through the blood-perfecting faith of the Lord Jesus.

As I read this, I heard the Lord Jesus say to me: *"Nancy, now is the time to receive My anointing for this commission. Enter into My rest. Enter into My faith. Receive the same spirit of these just men made perfect. Possess the land!"*

Suddenly, I saw myself in a vision walking down a long gallery in the Hall of Faith. There were all the saints of the ages, portrayed in paintings! I realized that my picture was already there, included among the just.

The Lord wants you in that Faith Hall of Fame, too. He has already made the provision for you to be there through Christ. The danger, warns verse 16, is that even born-again Christians can sell their spiritual birthright just as Esau did! Not all choose to be overcomers!

Third, there is a great urgency about receiving the Caleb anointing now. I learned this while presenting the Caleb message to a small group in Coleman. We were all worshipping in one accord. As I stood to exhort, all simultaneously received this anointing. One by one the Holy Spirit began to overwhelm us.

Soon, not a soul was left standing. Many were on their knees. Others fainted and lay as dead. We were experiencing a modern visitation like you read about during the first Great Awakening revivals of Whitefield and Finney.

As we laid on the floor before the Lord, overcome by the awesome visitation of God the Holy Spirit, a word of prophecy came forth from the Lord:

> *"I am calling. I am calling. Who will hearken to My call? I am giving instructions for these end-times. Who will listen? I am looking for My army to be strong in My Spirit and My Word. Who will answer the call?*
>
> *"For now is the time to receive the anointing and spirit to possess the land. Go in My name and save the people from the fire while there is still time.*

"Do you not recognize My army? It is made up of many people from all over the world. They have the name of Jesus as their head.

"Many people will ask, 'Who are these people with all power to set the captives free?' They will answer, 'Jesus is our head, and we are the body. He points the way to our Father, the almighty God.'"

I believe the time for receiving the Caleb anointing is now. This is our day to experience victorious service and possess the land. The Holy Spirit is opening new doors of service on your block and around the world!

Don't shrink back from entering in and going all the way with God. The Lord wants you to share in the victories of Caleb and the other heroes of faith. He wants you to join in creative intercession for the end-times move of God in your environs. Imagine what will happen as thousands of men and women discover that God has gifted them with the spirit of Caleb!

Now is the time to listen to the trumpet call and seize your inheritance! Together, we are about to see a final, great spiritual awakening in which millions will be saved and set free.

The Sin of Cowardice

Is it possible, I suppose, that some will read this and pull back. Fear and pride kept the Israelites from entering the promised land. Now is the time to release the childlike faith buried deep in your heart! Deliberately set aside your skepticism and receive all God has for you.

The cowardly and unbelieving will be thrown first into the lake of fire along with murderers, sorcerers and liars. (See Revelation 21:8.) Cowardice is not just another emotion, but a sin that needs to be confessed and forsaken. We must not shrink back from anything God has for us.

Although I hadn't realized it until that snowy night in Coleman, from time to time I had already been moving in and out of the Caleb anointing. For over twenty years —all the way back to the Billy Graham Crusade days—I had experienced flashes of Caleb power. I tasted it before I knew what to call it.

Perhaps you too have already experienced seasons of unusual, supernatural boldness, times when you have enjoyed the strength to conquer new territories for God in your life and witness. I believe this anointing ebbs and flows through disuse or use. Just as our muscles and even our brains weaken without exercise, so faith falters unless it is constantly challenged.

Stirring Up Our Gifts

Paul was probably talking about the same thing when he warned Timothy he must continually stir up the gift of the Holy Spirit which had been given to him by laying on of hands. We never arrive. We must always be moving forward and exercising our faith.

Having the spirit of Caleb is not a rank or badge of honor. It confers no degree or status that makes you into a super-saint, one suddenly more educated, gifted or talented than others. It is simply a tool that is no use unless it is used to birth and create the spiritual future.

If courage and obedient faith do not characterize your spiritual life, why not end this book by turning to the Lord and saying "yes" to the Holy Spirit? Ask the Lord Jesus Christ to help you begin to possess the land of promise He has provided for His bride, the church. If you have never joined Caleb's band, why not get on your face before the Lord right now and ask for the spirit of Caleb in your life and ministry? The Lord will grant what you ask for, the same anointing that followed Caleb—a spirit of dynamic, obedient faith which motivated him to courage and leadership. If you've walked in the Caleb spirit occasionally but have not been using it lately, ask the Lord to renew it today so you can possess your rightful inheritance in Christ.

Are you joining me, my dear potential Caleb, or will you fall in the wilderness with the unbelievers? By exercising this fresh anointing from God, you too can become a spiritual activist for Christ. If not, you'll find yourself forever unfulfilled and defeated in your Christian life.

As the Lord Jesus commanded in Acts 1:8, we are to reach out to the ever-widening circles of our own Jerusalems, Judeas, Samarias and to the ends of the earth. He promised we would do greater works than His. Everything He said will happen.

Start fresh today by asking the Father for the nations He has set aside for you and for the anointing of Caleb to be able to possess the land that is your inheritance.

A Prayer for the Caleb Anointing

Father God, giver of all good promises, grant me for Jesus sake the same spirit of faith and obedience you gave Caleb. May I possess my inheritance in Christ Jesus and follow you fully, too. Amen.